THE
NORTH
END
LIVES

THE NORTH END LIVES

A Journey Through Poverty Terrain

HUGO NEUFELD

Herald Press

Scottdale, Pennsylvania
Waterloo, Ontario

Hively Ave Mennonite Church
800 East Hively Ave
Elkhart, IN 46517

Library of Congress Cataloging-in-Publication Data
Neufeld, Hugo, 1940-
    The North End lives : a journey through poverty terrain / Hugo
Neufeld.
        p. cm.
    Includes bibliographical references (p.   ).
    ISBN 0-8361-9333-4 (pbk. : alk. paper)
    1. Church work with the poor—Ontario—Hamilton. 2. Church work
with the poor—Mennonites. 3. Neufeld, Hugo, 1940-   .   I. Title.
BV639.P6N48 2006
277.13'520829—dc22

2005037758

THE NORTH END LIVES
Copyright © 2006 by Herald Press, Scottdale, Pa. 15683
    Published simultaneously in Canada by Herald Press,
    Waterloo, Ont. N2L 6H7. All rights reserved
Library of Congress Catalog Card Number: 2005037758
International Standard Book Number: 0-8361-9333-4
Printed in the United States of America
Book design by Sandra Johnson
Cover by Sans Serif

12 11 10 09 08 07 06   10 9 8 7 6 5 4 3 2 1

To order or request information, please call
1-800-759-4447 (individuals); 1-800-245-7894 (trade).
Web site: www.heraldpress.com

To Doreen,
my loving wife and partner in ministry,
who travels with me on the journey of faith.
Together we have discovered the enormous richness
in people who lack financial resources
yet demonstrate an amazing capacity
to maneuver through poverty situations.

Contents

Foreword

One of the core problems in trying to respond effectively to the crisis of poverty is that we often don't see those who are poor. Our society segregates those who are materially secure from those who are struggling to get by. Societal forces have converged to create inner-city ghettos, trapping whole communities in isolation and marginalization. Meanwhile, many North Americans are victims of suburban blinders, safe in our comfortable and functioning lives, separated from our sisters and brothers who are poor.

In the absence of authentic human contact and relationship, we succumb to myths about the poor. Consciously or unconsciously, we come to accept that they are the victims of their own irresponsibility, and start to believe that men and women in poverty are morally flawed, and that their social circumstances are the consequences of character defects. Stereotypes of the poor as lazy, unproductive, criminal, or addicted go unchallenged. Perhaps even worse, those who are poor become invisible.

Hugo Neufeld has done a tremendous service. In this rich and deeply compassionate book, he *sees* those who are poor. He takes off his blinders—and ours. In moving with his family to the North End of Hamilton, Ontario, he chooses—or, to put it another way, is moved by God's Spirit—to enter into flesh and blood relationships. Through his presence and ministry, he comes to intimately know men, women, and children who are often rendered invisible. He transcends the myths and stereotypes and sees people for the wonderful and miraculous persons they are.

But these are not ordinary relationships. Because of the

social context of poverty, the men, women, and children of the North End put Neufeld in touch with deep human vulnerability and frailty. Our society often values people based on their success and productivity. Their dignity is bound up with material accomplishments and belongings. Poverty forces us to strip that veil away. The gift of poverty, if we dare to put it that way, is that it makes us confront the stark truth that suffering is a universal and inescapable part of being human, and that we cannot be fully human until we embrace the truth of suffering. But mysteriously, in seeing this truth of human vulnerability, we are also empowered to see more clearly the authentic worth and sacred dignity of each person. Neufeld's friendships in the North End teach him this fuller vision of what it means to be human.

I have been graced with this truth in my thirty years of working with persons who are homeless and disabled. The men and women I have known continue to teach me what it means to be human. They teach me about my own gifts, my own dignity.

But I have also come to believe that the men, women, and children who sleep on our streets and live in communities devastated by poverty are a prophetic presence: they affirm that something is radically wrong in our society. Hugo Neufeld has a similar testimony. As we follow him on his journey into the heart of the North End, we witness his deepening understanding not only of the personal struggles to survive, but of the social context of poverty. He comes to see with ever-greater clarity the structural and systemic factors that trap families and individuals in situations of scarcity and injustice. Through his eyes, we begin to understand the myriad forces that dehumanize and oppress those who are poor. And, like Neufeld, we are moved to work for change.

The North End Lives is ultimately a spiritual journey. Through his immersion in this remarkable community, Neufeld grasps the gospel mystery of God's love for and presence among those who are poor. His life becomes a witness to the upside-down Kingdom that Jesus proclaims, where holiness is present even in the harshest of circumstances, and where blessings abound in the midst of human struggle.

This book is the best kind of theology—an incarnational theology that is rooted in relationships, encounters, and stories. Neufeld's theology is about the biblical call for justice and shalom that brings about wholeness for all persons. Reading *The North End Lives*, we get a glimpse of that justice and shalom: an invitation to a restored human community, where each person's dignity is affirmed, where each person is allowed to flourish. By the risky choice of moving to a poor neighborhood, Neufeld has come to know this truth, and it has set him free. May the truth set us free as well.

> *Sister Mary Scullion, RSM*
> *Executive Director of Project H.O.M.E.*
> *Philadelphia, Pennsylvania*
> *Lent 2006*

Acknowledgments

What a rich adventure to interact with friends living below the poverty line who have offered so much to our entire family. To all of you, we express our gratitude. As we have authentically come to know each other in relationships that have moved toward mutuality, we have realized that all have gifts to share and weaknesses to be addressed. What we experienced has been powerful and life-changing for our family, and the generosity of those experiencing poverty has been uplifting.

North Enders who read these pages will recognize themes and experiences that have been so much a part of their lives. In many ways, you who are living or have lived below the poverty line could readily document the times of beauty and the experiences of harshness. You all deserve a big North End hug.

A whole-hearted thank-you to Joyce Lichtenberger for her contribution. During a vulnerable period in her life when she and her husband, Perry, were unemployed, the couple became actively involved at the center. Among the gifts they brought were Joyce's poetry and songwriting, complemented by Perry's guitar accompaniment. I am touched by her response after she reviewed the parts of this manuscript that included her songs. "There is an amazing sense of love and protection that washes over me as I read these words and relive these memories. Thank you for remembering my family with love; thank you for sharing these beautiful moments and lessons with others and giving them a chance to be an instrument of God's peace. Please know the 'fire' I felt burning burns strong today."

Our four sons, Gerald, Timothy, Sheldon, and Jonathan, who grew up in the North End, deserve commendation. Being the ages you were, you had little choice but to come along with us our quest to be a Christian presence in a setting you may not have chosen for yourselves. Thank you for your patience, your understanding, and your willingness to enter fully into the life of the community. I am also grateful for your comments and support as I shared with you the stories I was writing.

A very special thanks to Doreen. As codirector of the center and copastor of the church, she shared many of the stories in this book with me. In addition, she has her own unique, powerful experiences that could easily fill a second book. Her support, encouragement, and gentle nudges over the almost two decades we spent in the North End helped me to learn to appreciate the wonderful God who is present in all situations. In addition, her counsel and keen sense of detail in editing this manuscript have been invaluable in bringing about my dream of documenting the remarkable stories of which I was privileged to be a part.

The many staff, students, colleagues, and volunteers we worked with over the years all helped me to grow in leadership. Generous recognition must be given to the hundreds of Voluntary Service Workers (VSers) with whom we worked over the years. In writing this book I re-experienced many staff meetings in which we became very real with one another. There we theologized and planned programs, agonized over how to deal with community situations on our doorsteps, jested light-heartedly at our foibles, and found deep satisfaction in being part of a Christian community that was missional in its very essence.

Mennonite organizations, including Hamilton Mennonite Church, Mennonite Church Eastern Canada, Mennonite Church Canada, and Mennonite Church USA, have all been important to me. In addition, various other faith communities and social organizations have given us support.

To a loving God who brings meaning to life, I give thanks, acknowledging God's presence throughout my life.

A book such as this is influenced by many people. Especially in this past year, many of you have allowed me to test out the direction it was taking. In particular I want to express my gratitude to the readers of this manuscript, Brice Balmer, Arthur Paul Boers, and Sue Steiner, who provided helpful suggestions, and to Levi Miller and Michael Degan from Herald Press, who guided me through the process of completing it. My interaction with Marvin Friesen, the current pastor of Welcome Inn Church, and Donna Jean Forster, the executive director of Welcome Inn Community Center, was beneficial in giving me perspective. May these stories be an inspiration and a catalyst for the rich and the poor to unite with each other in life-giving relationships of mutuality.

Preface

Walking to the Welcome Inn Community Center one morning, I noticed that Bennetto Middle School, adjacent to our center, had received some fresh graffiti. Neatly spray-painted in bold letters were the words "The North End Lives." I generally lamented this type of street art, but this phrase caught my attention. Here was a slogan about the North End that conveyed a proud identity. To me it suggested vitality and growth and health. Is God not actively working in the oldest section of the city of Hamilton, as in every other neighborhood?

Over the years, negative stereotypes of the North End have been encouraged by the sad facts portrayed in headlines such as "North End Nightmare"; "Asthma Rate Triple in North End"; "Tougher for North Enders to Get Mortgages"; "16-Year-Old North Ender Wounded by Blast." Rare was a caption like the one that appeared in the December 11, 1999, issue of the *Hamilton Spectator*, which highlighted at least one positive quality:

> The northern end of Hamilton is a complex mix of grit and gritty characters, tough problems, and big-hearted neighbors.

In spite of the numerous problems that face the older cores of North American cities, we cannot forget the strengths of persons who live below the poverty line, strengths such as their generosity and care for one another. Over and over I've experienced the *big-hearted* love of North End friends. The stories shared in these pages, though unique to the North End of Hamilton, Ontario, are like those unfolding wherever poverty exists.

It is not easy to know how to refer to people living in poverty without some form of labeling that may carry negative connotations. I have chosen to use the term "North Ender" because the North End is the geographical area in which we ministered, and poverty was one of its unique characteristics. I generally use the designation "North Ender" to include those living in the oldest section of Hamilton, known as the North End. It is bounded by Lake Ontario's Hamilton Bay on the north and west, and a major Canadian National railway line on the south. I must point out that not all who live in the North End live below the poverty line. As the waterfront is reclaimed and older buildings are replaced with moderate and higher-end homes, people in poverty are losing their homes and being forced out of the neighborhood.

In these pages I invite you to hear the voices of North Enders and allow their giftedness to touch your soul. As I relived these precious events through my writing, I was often profoundly moved. On one occasion I burst into tears—a mixture of the sad and the joyful. For the next half-hour I was taken in by the mystery of the Holy Other. At the same time, it seemed as if Jesus the carpenter were sitting beside me at my desk, so close that I could have touched his clothing. I was reminded that the God who gave breath to all of us, bestowing on every person that special image-of-God heritage, looks at people of all economic and social backgrounds as children of God.

To respect our North End friends' privacy, the stories here at times represent a composite. I've changed some names and modified the facts of some events.

In July 1971, my wife, Doreen, and our three children—five-year-old Gerald, three-year-old Tim, and one-year-old Sheldon (our fourth son, Jonathan, was born in Hamilton three years later)—left our upwardly mobile lifestyle in British Columbia and moved into the North End. Doreen was an elementary school teacher by profession and I had been employed as a social worker. We sold our modest home in what everyone considered to be one of the better areas of town and used the money to purchase a ninety-five-year-old house in inner-city Hamilton, close to a public housing project. The reason for our transition was a strong inner call to use our gifts and experiences in a Mennonite Voluntary Service assignment.[1]

Our specific placement was to give leadership to a community center called the Welcome Inn, which had been opened a few years earlier by Hamilton Mennonite Church. In our first year, one of the strong supporters of the ministry said to me, "You'll be here a couple of years but then you'll move on to a regular job." I agreed with him. After all, our contract was only for a year, with the possibility of extending for a second year. But we fell in love with the area, the people, and the ministry, and frequently caught ourselves saying, "This is the best time to be at Welcome Inn." After three years, our status changed to salaried codirectors.

During the eighteen years that we served at the center, we saw many programs develop, including supportive ministries for all age groups, women's sewing classes, family outings, children's clubs, an emergency food bank, gardening projects, tutoring, counseling, and literacy and English as a second language classes. Various advocacy activities spoke to the issue of justice, including organizing those who were poor and working with local community groups to improve the social quality of a neighborhood. These all became an essential part of the overall work.

As the center grew, it moved from a narrow storefront to

a large home with a walkout basement, and then to its current location in a sizable former Baptist church. With the warm support and ongoing involvement of Hamilton Mennonite Church, the partnership expanded to include the Mennonite conferences, other denominations, social agencies, businesses, and governments. But the center kept its basic mandate to be a Christian presence.

As a strong service and social action ministry established itself, a worshipping faith community gradually emerged at the center. We will never forget the excitement as several local people helped replace the old sign that read, "Welcome Inn, A Community Friendship Center," with a new one with the added words "and Church." During one of those early services, with forty-seven worshipers present, former codirector Margarete Ediger voiced the wonder many were feeling when she began her sermon by saying, "Who would have thought that out of the old green sewing table would emerge a pulpit?" Indeed, in a natural, unforced way, through an emphasis on friendship and service, many had come to faith in Christ and were actively participating in the new worship community.

From our first days in Hamilton, Doreen and I worked as a team. This meant recognizing each other's gifts, encouraging each other in our growth, allowing each other space, learning new patterns of making decisions in a spirit of mutuality, and much more. North Enders readily affirmed our separate strengths, as well as the gifts we brought jointly.

What an exciting journey it has been! The commissioning service early in our ministry by Hamilton Mennonite Church was encouraging to us. Several years later, with the additional support and involvement of the local community and the wider church, we were each ordained to strengthen our service in the newly developing congregation. Today we are still working as a team in a part-time pastoral assignment. Thanks be to God!

Come now, and gently tread through these pages, allowing the Holy One to help you see Jesus through friends who know all about poverty. As the North End lives, allow yourself to live also. Thrilling reign-of-God surprises await.

-1-
Eye Openers

"And whoever gives even a cup of cold water to one of these little ones in the name of a disciple—truly I tell you, none of these will lose their reward." *(Matthew 10:42)*

The kingdom is full of surprises. Again and again in parables, sermons and acts, Jesus startles us. Things are not like they are supposed to be. The stories don't end as we expected. The Good Guys turn out to be the Bad Guys. The ones we expected to receive a reward get spanked. Things are reversed. Paradox, irony, and surprise permeate the life of Jesus. The least are the greatest. The immoral receive forgiveness and blessing. Adults become like children. The religious miss the heavenly banquet. The pious receive curses. Things are just not like we think they should be. We are baffled, perplexed, and most of all surprised. We are caught off guard. We step back in amazement. We aren't sure if we should laugh or cry. The kingdom surprises us again and again by turning our world upside down.[2] —*Donald B. Kraybill*

A Cup Filled to the Brim

It was one of those hot, humid, stifling summer days in southern Ontario. Through an extended heat wave, the seasoned bricks and mortar on our century-old house, like other houses in the North End, heated the neighborhood to an exhausting temperature. Air-conditioning was out of our price range. This was one of those times I felt trapped living in the inner city.

"Just get me out of here!" I felt like screaming. A dozen kilometers of smokestacks and steel factories representing prosperity for the well-to-do separated me from the cool but blemished blue waters of Lake Ontario. Was I not called to serve in this oldest area of Hamilton with all its poverty? Didn't that mean walking with those who are poor, even on hot summer days? And had I not specifically promised to visit Conrad?

This cheerful but poorly dressed young lad of seven years had come to the Welcome Inn Community Center, where I served. He had been there several times, demonstrating premature parenting skills with his younger brother and sister. One day as he gazed at the center's momentarily open fridge, with all its abundance, Conrad had softly but passionately said, "I wish our fridge was like that!" Like others I knew, his family didn't have enough food to eat.

I was finally ready to put together several grocery bags of good, nutritious food and be on my way. A look at the address confirmed my suspicion: Conrad lived in a dilapidated, crime-prone area at the edge of the North End. I thought, "I don't want to go there. Isn't that close to where the Wentworth

Street gang hangs out? It's not the safest place in the world. Why not call the family to meet me at the center? But they have no vehicle."

Finally, I decided to go. My fears were overridden by a strong motivation to help—or was it the encouragement of the holy God I served?

I finally located Conrad's home, and it was what I had guessed. Greeting me was a partially boarded-up, one-story building, with a railway track on one side and a grungy run-down tavern on the other. On all sides the steel companies pressed in, spewing out industrial waste through rusting smokestacks. "No family should ever be forced, or even allowed, to live in such an unhealthy place," I thought.

As I knocked on a door that seemed to have been wedged crudely into the frame with a crowbar, I heard a familiar voice. "Come on in."

Conrad invited me into the sweltering house. Not a single fan was anywhere in sight, let alone air-conditioning. Making my way over the patchwork of missing floor tiles, I could see that someone had tried to do hasty repair jobs, using whatever materials might be available, even if incongruent with normal building standards. A few dim light bulbs glared at me; there were no glass fixtures. Plaster was falling from the ceiling, exposing a leaky roof. A thick, foul, pungent odor that spoke of broken pipes and a clogged sewer engulfed my sensitive, middle-class nostrils. I could hear water dripping; no, it was close to running. A glance into the kitchen told me it was coming from the sink faucet, where water was sprinkling on overturned dishes. With virtually no cupboard space, pots and pans and eating utensils were sprawled over the limited counter space. I wondered what landlord in good conscience could put such a house up for rent.

Conrad's mother graciously invited me to the table, where she was neatly folding the freshly laundered but still-stained sheets, shirts, and pants. A daughter of about five was trying out her skill in precisely tucking in the loose ends to make sure the tower of clothes wouldn't fall over, while another son, maybe two, squirmed in an old-fashioned high chair, playing with some string.

"We were homeless," Conrad's mother told me. "But now we at least have a place to live. It's the best we can afford. I'm trying to fix this place up. Yesterday I scrubbed the floor for hours, but the tiles just keep coming off. I'm sorry we only have one small window that opens. The landlord nailed the others shut, so we have to put up with the heat."

She obviously was making the best of her situation. A stream of hope and optimism rippled through the relentless, impossible hour-to-hour and day-to-day frustrations that this family was surely encountering. I couldn't imagine myself in such circumstances, and I quickly concluded that at one time she also would have felt that way.

Like a hard-working asphalt street paver on a sizzling day, I found myself perspiring profusely. Yet it was not only because of the extreme heat in the house. Overpowering me from every side were the images of poverty. "Poverty makes me uncomfortable," I thought. "Something is not right. A God of love could not intend it to be this way."

Suddenly I saw Conrad, with those innocent, brown eyes, smiling and looking straight up at me. In a clear, gentle voice he asked, "Would you like a cup of cold water?"

My instinctive, impulsive, unspoken reaction was negative. "No way, not in this place. Let me out of here. Give me some breathing room."

But something was beginning to stir deep down in my being. Was it a miracle?

My preoccupation with the physical surroundings and my own comfort began to be replaced with the beauty of a child's caring. With a nudge from that ultimate energy Source, I couldn't help but be touched by his heart-and-soul offer, so I said, "That would be great."

Out of the corner of my eye, I saw Conrad go to the kitchen, carefully wash out a dollar-store glass, dry it with a blue, patterned tea towel, open the almost empty fridge, and select an extra-large ice cube. From the ever-leaking faucet he filled the cup to the brim and slowly carried it, offering a few wet drops to the uneven floor tiles. With an enormous smile on his face, he presented me with the crystal-clear cup of cold water.

The words of Jesus came to me: "Whoever gives even a cup of cold water to one of these little ones in the name of a disciple—truly I tell you, none of these will lose their reward" (Matthew 10:42). Suddenly I was gripped by this sermon incarnated into my life.

Still clutched in my hand were the grocery bags of food. I had come to give, to respond to needs, but I was the one receiving. I had come to feed the hungry, but I was the one being fed. I had come with all my social work, counseling, and friendship resources, but I was the one receiving hospitality. I could respond only by drinking deeply of the water of life.

So You Want to Be a North Ender

There was a scuffle at the entrance to the storefront on 428 James Street North. This long, narrow building, with its indented entrance between two storefront windows, served as a drop-in center ministry of Hamilton Mennonite Church. Numerous old shops still sprinkled the main thoroughfare through the old North End, in various stages of urban renewal. Five energetic teens were vying to be first through the door. Heading straight for me at the back of the room, they ignored my conversation on the phone and encircled me as if pouncing on prey.

Claude, obviously the leader, blurted out, "You're the new guy here. You're going to be our club leader."

Excitedly but cautiously interrupting him, Shane explained, "You'll be taking us to all kinds of places. You've got your license; you've got the keys to the van; let's go to Webster's Falls."

Yes, I was new. The introduction to my one-year voluntary service assignment had been brief; it included a tour of the area, meeting a few people from the community, and being introduced to members of the supporting congregation. In retrospect, I realize how little I knew about putting my professional social-work skills into practice. At that point, however, I remained naively confident.

Almost losing my cool, and at best somewhat defensive, I retorted, "Back off, guys, I'm making this important call. How about coming back tomorrow, let's say, 4 p.m.?"

Roy, the shortest of the bunch, pressed forward and tried to explain things in a more logical way. "We came here last year and that Menno, he was a pretty good guy. But he's gone now. So you're the one."

Showing a bit of cleverness, Darcy, characterized by an obvious facial disfiguration, remarked, "You've got that sign up in the window. It says, 'Meet Your Friends Here,' and that's what we are doing."

By then, one of the teens had grabbed the phone out of my hand and hung it up. I was at the mercy of the five, some of the tough street teens of the North End. No one else was at the center. Suddenly, I was feeling stripped of all my resources, and my heart sank.

Had I ever been this powerless and, yes, helpless? I couldn't think of one example in my five years as a social worker to compare with this one. In my textbook training, as well as in the practical field placements at the Clarke Institute of Psychiatry and the Family Service Agency, we had been taught to keep a professional distance from our clients. But nothing in my studies, no amount of role paying or writing up or analyzing numerous interviews had prepared me for this encounter. What was I to do?

I was still in shock when Claude sat down on one of the short, homemade, foam-padded cheese barrels that surrounded a low, round table. "Come on, boys, let's talk." He invited all to take a seat.

I thought, "Who's in charge?"

Claude grabbed the phone pad with my half-written note and shoved it at me. "Let's make a list of what we want to do this year," he said. I noticed that the others responded to Claude's aggressive leadership and seemed to settle down.

I was still very intimidated but tried to cover up my frustration. I managed to speak in a relatively calm voice. "Look, guys, I'll consider being your leader, but first I want to know more about you. Tell me your names and what you enjoy doing. What's it like to live in the North End?"

That began an interesting conversation in which I not only got to know the fellows a little better but also came to understand how our sign, "Meet Your Friends Here," needed to be taken seriously.

Claude, Shane, and Roy were all from single-parent families who lived in the Survey, across the road from the center. The one-story, geared-to-income housing project covered two blocks and was part of a massive urban renewal project in the North End. The hastily built family units were bunched together, with no windows in the basements and almost no play area. Nevertheless, with the expropriation of hundreds of older low-rental houses that had graced the area, many families on fixed incomes had found suitable accommodation in the Survey. At the same time, there was a stigma attached to the project. The city's newspapers referred to it as the "North End ghetto." Survey kids sometimes reveled in a self-fulfilling prophecy as a tough bunch, and our three adventurous adolescents were no exception.

There was also Medi, who lived in an old clapboard house overlooking the bay. He and his friends would skip out of school for an afternoon of fun at the waterfront. He was the expert who was able to bypass security people at the steel factories and private yacht clubs. Some of his interest in this activity no doubt came from his father, a union man who worked on the docks unloading ships. His mother spent long hours selling real estate. With little supervision, Medi sometimes spent more time on the streets than in the classroom.

Finally, there was Darcy, who had to go to a special school outside the North End because he was, as the others put it, "a slow guy." While other kids often picked on him, this group offered him protection.

The orientation during my first official club evening was not quite the baptism I had expected. After our impromptu planning session, I cautiously agreed to meet with the boys on a weekly basis, beginning the next day. Emerging programs at the center included weekly clubs that offered constructive, healthy activities. Why not sign these fellows up?

The first session would be an evening of shooting pool in the center's basement, where we had a beat-up table that had been donated to us. Various items competed for space beside the pool table, including an old octopus-style furnace, shelves of used clothing, yard sale items, a food bank, sports equipment, craft supplies, a squished bathroom, and some old couches.

When the guys came in, I immediately escorted them to the basement, where the first game went rather well. "This is going to be fun," I thought. I had thoroughly prepared a host of creative ideas so that when the boys got restless I could introduce a new set of activities. The problem with one of those was that four of them had to watch, while the other tested his skills. This more individualistic game eventually led to a kind of bedlam, where the boys took free rein of the basement. Tag took on a new dimension for me when the young men added an uncontrollable hide-and-seek element.

Relief finally came when Claude, exhausted from his running around, discovered the food bank supplies. "Hey, guys, look what's here!"

While I protested, he proceeded to open a jar of donated homemade dill pickles and share them in communion-like fashion with everyone, including me. This scene was almost humorous to me for a moment. Pulling out the biggest dill, Claude remarked, "This here represents the good times we are going to have as a club, and cheers to our leader." With that, I found myself munching on a morsel that had never carried such meaning for me. Into the mix of thoughts and emotions rang words I had intellectually debated at my Bible college:

Truly I tell you, just as you did it to one of the least of these who are members of my family, you did it to me. (*Matthew 25:40*)

But was I doing any good? Was not God calling me to serve? Who was helping whom?

Then one of the boys turned off the main power switch. Everything was a murky blackness. There were no cellar windows to give even a glimmer of light. I could hear the boys laughing as they tried to scare me. They knew the tapestry of the cellar better than I did. While I yelled for the lights to be put back on, I suddenly felt something wet and warm streaking down my pant leg. Could it be? No, it couldn't be. Yes, I smell it. It was pee! I was being urinated on.

This was more than I could bear. Saying I was ticked off is mild. I could think of other language I could have used, words that my North End friends were quite familiar with.

I was ready to quit. "Just take me back to my social-work office" I thought, "where I can practice counseling in a more predictable way." Holding back tears of frustration, but paying little attention to my anger that was ready to burst out, I mustered up all the authority I could and ushered the boys upstairs and out the front door.

"You can only come back after you apologize and agree to work out some ground rules," I yelled.

That evening and in the days to come I pondered my "baptism" to the North End of Hamilton. I had come there to be a Christian presence, which was the explicit mandate of our center. And I sincerely desired to live and work in the geographical location to which I felt God had called me. And, yes, I did want to become a North Ender and get to know people in the area from all age groups.

But the culture was so different from what I was used to. Could I really become a North Ender and identify with this section of the city, with its tradition of toughness? Already in my first years of social work I had embraced the principle that before you can earn the right to help, you must understand the people and the situation in which they live. I had experienced the roughness of teens whose values were dictated by the streets. I had also been tested to the limit that my practical Christian faith allowed me to go. My personal space had been violated!

In the end, my final outbursts of anger spoke with leadership power. I too had tough love, though it had been shaped in a vastly different climate. As I discovered later, my unguarded confrontation set the stage for some positive experiences with this group of teens.

But what about the pickles? I could see it as a theft; the guys had no right to raid the food bank. They should have asked for permission. But in the days ahead I soon discovered that North Enders are more concerned about sharing their resources than about storing them under lock and key. I had to admit that when Claude handed out those pickles, no one was excluded. All could partake of the resources that well-meaning people had donated.

Questions continued to circulate in my mind. Who is going to open the pickle jars, the resources that are so bountiful in our rich country? Who will risk themselves to open the tightly sealed lids? Who will unscrew the lids of untold wealth stashed away in corporations, governments, families, and even churches? Who will walk with the poor in their struggle for justice? And who has the keys to make sure all receive?

God, Why Are We Here?

After several years in a tiny two-story duplex, where the house including the front and back yards could easily have fit into my parents' newly built bungalow, we decided to find a bigger place in the same general area. Our "dream home" was a tall, two-story, hundred-year-old brick building on Simcoe Street. When Doreen and I and our four young sons moved in, a surprise awaited us. We soon learned that a motorcycle gang lived right across the street. When we saw these men on motorcycles with "Satan's Choice" written on their jackets slowing down in front of our house, our cry to God went something like this:

> Have we made the wrong choice after all? We thought we were improving our living situation. We're here to live and teach your love in this community, but you can't put our kids in danger. There's Gerald, our oldest, only ten; Tim, two years younger; Sheldon, just barely in school; and then there's one-year-old Jonathan. Should we have stayed in our middle-class neighborhood in British Columbia, where Doreen had a teaching job and I had good employment with a social agency? Would it have been wiser for us to remain in that "good" area, where we had purchased our first home on a hill overlooking the city?

We know we were well on in our upwardly mobile journey. Somehow, God, you gently shook us into making a change. But you also directed us to this particular place. There were so many signals for us to come to serve in this area of many needs. It was only to be a year or two, but now you have asked us to become more permanent. Some of our friends and relatives wonder how we can do it. They question whether we are fair to our children and to ourselves. But you called us. We dedicated our children to you and feel they will grow up learning to appreciate all cultures and people. But a biker gang that can penetrate into our living space and revved-up motorcycles that can hassle our vulnerable children? How can you do this to us?

It didn't help to hear that there was a biker war going on. A number of bombings had resulted in several deaths.

For the next while, we simply kept to our side of the narrow street and had no confrontations and no interactions with them, except for the noise of their super-powered bikes cruising into their driveway. Keeping distance is the way to go, we thought. We won't bother them and they won't bother us. Yet we still had the uneasy feeling that somewhere our family could be caught in the crossfire. We could not deny our close proximity to these notorious neighbors.

One day one of the neighborhood boys who was part of our youth program came over and asked me to help him get his small motorbike started. Mario was fifteen years old and had often been treated like someone on the other side of the tracks. Come to think of it, we were all literally living on "the other side of the tracks," because a major train line, the Canadian National Railway, separated the North End community from the rest of Hamilton.

"Sure, I'll see if I can get your bike going."

Confidently, I tried everything I could think of. I took out the spark plug and cleaned it, checked the fuel line, adjusted the carburetor, but try what I would, nothing worked.

In frustration Mario suddenly blurted out, "Who around here knows something about motorcycles anyway?"

Somewhat facetiously, I said, "There's Satan's Choice across the street."

"Well, let's go," Mario said confidently.

I wasn't so sure, but before I knew it he had grabbed my arm and I was reluctantly helping him push his motorbike up the small incline to the back of the large house across the street, where the Satan's Choice "brothers" lived. In the backyard we found ourselves surrounded by at least a dozen motorcycle people, all profusely drinking beer. I hadn't known that there was a tent trailer behind the house, which expanded their living space and served as a kind of headquarters during the summer months.

One of the biggest, huskiest guys—they all seemed big to me, in contrast to my mere 145 pounds on a six-foot frame—with his muscle shirt and tattooed arms, came up to me and challenged, "What do you want?"

"I'm just a neighbor; can you help my friend with his bike?" I timidly managed to say.

Crossing his huge arms into an X, he leaned back and began to survey the circle of members, who by unspoken command immediately looked up from their partying.

I didn't know what to expect. "Mario, what have you got me into?" I thought. "I've got to get myself out of this mess, and quickly."

The boss looked over his gang as he pivoted his 350 pounds and pointed at one of the junior members. "Hey, kid, you fix the bike."

Without a hint of hesitation the young man went to work. In a few minutes the bike was actually running. It seemed like a miracle. Mario was ecstatic and roared his bike down the street and out of sight. I noticed just a twinkle of a smile and a sense of satisfaction in the expression of the Satan's Choice leader. I said a quick thank-you to the people I did not really want to associate with and hurriedly left.

That night I felt a certain amount of inner affirmation. I had begun to establish a relationship with the neighbors. Remarkably, it had not been my initiative to get involved and it had gone better than expected.

I had read Don Kraybill's book *The Upside-Down Kingdom* and had been intrigued by the surprises that Jesus gave his disciples through his teaching and life actions. Phrases from the book jogged back to me: "The kingdom of God is full of surprises . . . Jesus startles us . . . Good Guys turn out to be the Bad Guys . . . The least are the greatest . . . The religious miss the heavenly banquet . . . Things are just not like we think they should be . . . The kingdom surprises us again and again by turning our world upside down."[3]

I wondered who were the good guys in my journey of that day and who were the bad guys?

Of one thing I was sure: Jesus had walked with me into what I perceived to be a den of lions and in that violent milieu I found compassion. Could God actually be at work in that shadowy household? The territory of God's actions that I had previously seen as primarily confined to the church was being expanded. Just as surprisingly, my neighborhood had suddenly become a little safer.

Not long after this encounter I heard that one of the Satan's Choice members had wiped out on his motorcycle on the Mary Street Bridge, which separated the North End from the rest of Hamilton. This CN track overpass had been built in the World War I era. Because of its steep hump in three sections, the bikers saw it as a challenge: who could traverse it fastest? North End rumor had it that Derrick, a new recruit to the gang, was a few blocks away at Hamilton General Hospital. The talk was that he was a mess, with multiple scrapes and broken bones.

I felt a Holy Spirit nudge to visit him. How would I find him? What was his last name? Using all the investigative skills I had learned from the streets, I finally found myself at Derrick's hospital room. But the door was closed, which seemed unusual.

Boldly, and perhaps foolishly, I opened the door without knocking and stepped in. There in front of me was a roomful of Goliath-size motorcycle people surrounding the bed. Again I felt intimidated; my legs transformed into jelly. One of the biggest guys turned to me and said, "What do you want?"

Fortunately, Derrick recognized me as a neighbor, and then it was like the parting of the Red Sea. Everybody stood back as the bandaged gang member, who was strung up in traction, ushered me to his bedside.

I don't recall much of the conversation, but I do remember that my presence was important to Derrick. Somehow, with my being there, he was able to reflect on some of the values in his life and the choices he was making. I suddenly realized that he was the young man who had fixed Mario's motorbike. "I enjoyed that," he said. "I'll gladly make someone happy."

He continued, "Our world needs more people who will help each other out. Yes, I know there is a God. Pray for me. Your visit means a lot. Thank you for coming."

No, Let Me Walk Home

I was feeling exceptionally generous and good after leading what I felt had been a successful men's group. Some of the men were beginning to take responsibility for shaping the programming, and many excellent leaders from the community were emerging for all the activities at the center. Doreen and I could see the day when we would no longer need to be in charge. In addition to the regulars, there had been a number of new fellows, including Joe. The word was getting around that this was a good place to come.

We had made some of our original, deep-fried donuts, enough for an afternoon coffee break plus half a dozen for each person to take home. As I was leaving the center, I could see Joe, whose disability caused him to limp, struggling to keep his wool coat together. The wind was blowing harshly, picking up loose snow. The late-afternoon temperature was beginning to dip well below freezing.

"I'll give you a ride home," I said. "I'll drop you off wherever you live."

Reluctant at first, Joe finally said, "Just take me up James Street to Wilson."

When we got close to the destination, I quizzed him on exactly which was his place. "It's cold, I'll take you right to the doorstep."

"No, just drop me off here."

The impulse of the good Samaritan (Luke 10:25-37) didn't

allow me to abandon him, so I pressed my invitation. He consented and I drove on, but the same thing happened. He asked to be let out, but I insisted on taking him to the front door.

After several more stops, he said, "We're here now. My place is just around the corner. I'm very okay. You be on your way."

By then I was really curious. Why in this windy, cold weather did he not want me to take him home? Where did this man live? We had passed through downtown and were at the edge of some century-old houses that had at one time been the luxury of Hamilton. After years of aging they had received their second wind through major renovations and were considered upscale. Was he wealthy? Could he be living in one of these? Did he have a family? I didn't know what to think.

As Joe began making his way down the street, he called back, "Good-bye, I'll see you next week at the men's group. I had such a good time today."

Still curious, I parked the car and followed him at a distance. He turned toward downtown and at the end of an alley slowly bent down to pass through an opening in the chain-link fence that separated the towering houses from the train tracks below. As I hurriedly made my way to the fence and leaned over, I saw Joe traverse through the tall weeds and then slip through an underpass. I followed to a point where I could still see him. Isolated from the bustling city overhead and the occasional train whistle below, nestled in a corner concrete abutment was a large cardboard box: home for Joe.

I was utterly astonished. He was homeless. It suddenly dawned on me that I had entered Joe's private territory. I was still in a shocked stupor when Joe reappeared. He glared at me in the distance, turned around, and walked the other way. I realized I had embarrassed him.

There was no sign of Joe at the next men's group. I felt guilty and could have kicked myself for my misplaced goodwill. I wanted to apologize and tell him I was sorry for pushing too hard and not respecting his wishes. I also wanted to convey some kind of regret for being part of a wealthy society in which low-cost housing is so scarce. I wanted to tell him that in my faith journey I was beginning to realize that I also have a responsibility to ensure that all have suitable housing.

To be sure, the good Samaritan impulse is what Joe needed. He had, to a certain degree, experienced the hospitality of the center through the men's activity and had been prepared to come back. But the compassion and calling to serve my neighbor did not give me permission to tread into his private space without his consent.

I never saw Joe again. His final look continued to haunt me in the search for fulfillment of Jesus's mandate to authentically and sensitively "go and do likewise."

The Day We Enjoyed a Roast Beef Dinner

I grew up in a relatively well-to-do farming family but had all kinds of questions about the rich and the poor. When I went to the big city to deliver produce, I wondered why there were so many dilapidated buildings with people actually living in them. Did God intend for children to grow up in crowded, rundown houses that should have been torn down long ago? I saw the increasing numbers of homeless on the streets and wondered why this should be. Why did we need soup kitchens and food banks in a country with so much wealth?

Not long after leaving the farm, I came across a pamphlet entitled "This Too Is Canada." The pictures and the description of the plight of the poor were disturbing, and I resolved to do something about such a disgraceful situation. I had been raised in a strong Christian Mennonite family and taught to share, help, serve, and give to those we called "less fortunate." We were to emulate Jesus, whom Paul quoted as saying, "It is more blessed to give than to receive" (Acts 20:35b).

I remember a university class in which it suddenly struck me that labeling persons as underprivileged was entirely one-sided. Wasn't there more to these people? Nothing seemed to be positive in such a definition. And then sometime later I heard the words "welfare recipient." Again this placed people in a derogatory and negative category. I had the nagging thought that all was not well when some of us could be bountiful givers while others were by definition "receivers." Taking on a service assignment and living in the neighborhood in which we worked had only increased my longing to make sense of it all.

I was to begin to get answers to some of the questions preoccupying my thoughts. It was not I, but a family of three, living below the poverty line, who took the initiative. They invited Doreen and me, together with Sheldon, our youngest son at the time, for supper in their home.

"We get our check tomorrow and I'd like to make a meal for you," Jerry eagerly explained. "Ada will help and, of course, I know how much Sheldon enjoys playing with Jakie."

My initial, unspoken response to such a surprising invitation was, "But you shouldn't have. Isn't it too much for you?" What I was really thinking was, "You always run out of food at the end of the month, and this will really cut you short." And I confess I did not have the confidence that this family could actually make a decent meal that I would enjoy.

The guilt-ridden response that came out verbally was the suggestion that we could invite them all to our house, where we had much more room. "Jakie and Sheldon can play with the new board game we just got him for his birthday." Later I wondered how the counter-invitation sounded to our friends, who had so warmly offered their hospitality. But we accepted the invitation—glad on the outside, reluctant on the inside.

Friday night came and we found ourselves timidly knocking on a shabby door leading down into a dingy part of a six-unit, 1950s apartment building. The door opened quickly; they were expecting us and graciously greeted us. "I'm so glad you've come," Ada said with her face beaming. "I just know we'll all enjoy ourselves."

Despite the crumbling, old-fashioned wallpaper and the broken linoleum floor coverings, there was a remarkable neatness in the house. Because there were few closets or cabinets, the ordinary supplies of the house were carefully stacked in various corners. The warm hugs we received from Jerry and

Ada suggested that I peel away some of my preconceived notions.

It was the delicious aroma that had already been trickling through the entrance that soon captivated our attention. With pride, Jerry carried into the room one of the finest, largest prime rib roasts we had ever seen. Other heaping dishes were brought to the table: a scrumptious health-food salad, steaming corn, mouth-watering cinnamon applesauce, dark-green dill pickles, oven-browned mashed potatoes, and thick gravy. I could hardly keep myself from blurting out, "But you've blown your whole welfare check!"

"Welcome again," Jerry said. "Sit here. I'm sorry we don't have enough chairs for everyone," and he opened the door of the tiny adjoining room and sat down on the bed that he had pulled into the doorway. "This way I can give you good service when you run out of food." I protested this kind of hospitality, but what could I offer? There wasn't enough furniture.

We thoroughly enjoyed the meal, and for a time I forgot the deep chasm economically and socially between us. We laughed a lot, with everyone participating in the storytelling. Whenever we so much as offered to help, we were quickly admonished, "No, you are our guests. We want to serve you."

I can still see the wonderful satisfaction that glistened in Jerry and Ada's eyes as we said farewell and thanked them for the wonderful evening. Many thoughts lingered in my mind. Uppermost was the conviction that I was on a journey to discover the wealth in those who are poor.

I Chose the Biggest Banana

I had been invited to lead the chapel service at the men's shelter down the road from our center. By then this historic "rescue mission" had been transformed in such a way that the altar-call sermon was not a prerequisite for receiving a meal. Years earlier, during my Bible-college years in Winnipeg, I had spent every Saturday night singing in a quartet at a rescue mission. Songs such as "Come ye disconsolate" had blared onto the streets through a screechy microphone.

While intentions were good, I was always bothered by a simplistic theology that placed an overwhelming emphasis on sin, evil, and bad behavior. Where was the God of love, whose inviting eyes would look beneath the surface to see the deep needs of these persons? What had brought such folk to live their lives on the street?

As I spent time getting to know the homeless, I discovered individuals discharged from psychiatric hospitals with few supports. Others were hampered with various other forms of disabilities that gave them little access to meaningful work. Some were simply unemployed. I wondered whether racial prejudices and discrimination played a part in keeping them on the street. More recently I had heard from an aboriginal North Ender how he had been so pleased to finally receive telephone confirmation of a place to live. But when the landlord saw him in person, his immediate comment was, "I can't rent to you." The awkward silence that followed was broken by the jarring, untruthful words, "This place is not for rent."

I agonized over what I could say in the chapel service that might touch the lives of those who sought shelter for the night. Finally, I decided to dispense with the usual preacher-style sermon and simply try to focus on the beauty of people and nature, all of which had been created by a loving God. I would show slides. Carefully, I selected the clearest pictures from our collection, close-ups of people of many backgrounds, people with joy on their faces and also a few with sadness, because that was also a reality. I would minimize any spiritualizing comments and instead simply try to portray the goodness at the heart of every person. To complete the portrait of this world, I would show some nature pictures—God's creation—including some taken right in the inner city.

I was surprised to see a good group of men who had chosen to come to chapel that day. Indeed, they showed a keen interest, especially when I began showing pictures of downtown, with which they were so familiar. At that point in my presentation, I had the attention of every man in the room. In the end, there was hearty applause.

With such a positive reception from the men, I decided to go down and have supper with them. As I was going past the front desk, one of the leaders glared at me. "That was not a sermon," he declared. "These men need Jesus." The criticism cut me to the bone, and I couldn't put those words out of my mind throughout the meal.

The dining area, which was in the basement, had very inferior, out-dated furnishings. The soup was lukewarm and watery, and I found it almost impossible to swallow. So I thought I'd have some coffee. That was brought in kettles that had obviously been standing around for a while. To make things even worse, sugar had already been added, and I've never liked sweetened coffee. Needless to say, I found my stomach churning from both the emotional stress and the second-rate food.

"If we are going to help people," I thought to myself, "why not have a decent meal for them." As soon as I could discreetly exit, I quickly did.

As I was leaving I noticed across the street a small grocery store with some inviting-looking fruit in the window. Without hesitation, I marched into the store, ripped out the largest banana I could find, paid the cashier, and before I was out of the store I found myself aggressively consuming it. Why in the world would I be doing this? For the next few days my experience of that day took center stage in my thinking and meditation.

I had been called to serve in the inner city as a Christian presence at the Welcome Inn Center. My mentor, Herman Enns, and the church behind this ministry, had strongly urged me to think of ministry in a holistic way. We were there to meet the physical, emotional, and spiritual needs of people, and before one could speak about faith, one needed to genuinely understand and love people. Before sermonizing, some helpful responses must be made to address their immediate needs, including all that results from alienation from most of society.

It was right and good for me to be willing to work with another church agency and help them out. To be honest and share the beauty of people in their chapel time seemed appropriate. It was gratifying to me that, in spite of the criticism, I was repeatedly invited to come back to speak. The agency knew that chapel time had to be more positive if it was going to reach the men. With more emphasis on God's love and grace, and without a prescribed formula, a faith discovery process could be set in motion, where even the most wounded person on the street could sense some hope. But I couldn't get over the meager, sloppy food that had been served. Perhaps it was a lack of resources.

From my first months at the center I realized how difficult it is to raise standards when there simply isn't the money to do it. I recalled how one of our denominational workers had responded to my hope that we would be able to replace our old, rusted, indoor garbage containers with new, large, plastic ones: "Surely our church conference has enough money to pay for trash containers," he had insisted. Unfortunately, at the next annual wider-church gathering, our budget was not increased. With inflation, a flat budget was actually a decrease, leaving us no room for upgrading.

Maybe this particular mission was also short of resources. Perhaps they had to use donated, deteriorating vegetables for the soup because money wasn't available. Or perhaps this was a situation where the cook, who had been hired off the street, had some problems. Could there have been conflicts in management? In any case, I knew something was inherently wrong when those who are poor are granted the cast-offs. What message were we giving to those who have few resources? In the Bible story of the poor man Lazarus (Luke 16:19-31), who sought only the crumbs that fell from the rich man's table, didn't Jesus clearly challenge those who feast sumptuously to remove the barriers between the rich and the poor on this earth? You cannot do this by giving only of your surplus or substandard items. I became determined to examine my donations and to begin challenging others to do the same.

But there was a discrepancy, a reaction perhaps. Why did I deliberately purchase the biggest banana to satisfy my hunger? I began to realize that when my physical needs were not met in the shelter, I had an alternative that allowed me to splurge. Could it be that I was meshed into a society where many of us can indulge at will, while our goodwill is simply the provision of leftovers? Such a pattern, I pondered, might contribute to polarizing our society in such a way that those who are poor will stay poor. Surely this could not be God's intention.

I'll Sue You

What a great day to be alive! We had received a donation of $2,000 from a single man who was a long-distance trucker. In his letter he told us how he had been moved to compassion when he had visited the center and had talked to some of the people from the neighborhood. His commitment to his employer prevented him from entering voluntary service. Instead, he chose to live on a basic allowance similar to voluntary service while continuing his job. This would allow him to contribute substantial amounts of money to the Welcome Inn every year.

Other positives happened that day. The Wednesday afternoon women's group, led by Doreen, was filled to capacity in response to a volunteer who had offered to help each woman make a pair of jeans. A family counseling session with two teens and their parents had brought about an amazing reconciliation. I was feeling good, tiptoeing on top of the world, and since it was my turn to make the evening meal, I announced to Doreen that supper would be late, but it would be one of my classic banquet suppers. She could spend time with our four sons, playing games in the family room.

I closed the door of the kitchen and worked steadily for the next hour and a half at the meal, improvising the recipes in the process. I decided to proceed with a version of curried steak I had made before. At the same time, I began to work on a variety of Asian-type dishes with veggies that needed just the right amount of cooking time to retain their flavor and color. Fresh blueberry pie and ice cream would complete the meal. While remaining attentive to all four stove elements and the precise timing each dish called for, I brought out the candles, tablecloth, and our finest plates, bowls, goblets, and cutlery. With all the pressures facing us from day to day, this time of family interaction around a candle-light dinner served as a refuge from all the cares out there.

Gerald talked about his new interest in model rockets. He and several friends had plans to invite our entire congregation to a rocket-launching demonstration at the Royal Botanical Gardens after church. Tim was excited about his perfect mark in math, along with a nice note he had received from his teacher. Sheldon begged us to get him some hockey cards for his birthday. Jonathan chattered about his new motorized dump truck, which we had picked up at a yard sale. By the end of supper, the excitement and pace of the conversation had ratcheted to a high level. Even with the few inevitable skir-mishes, the good evening was climaxing an excellent day. I felt rewarded for my efforts. My, how blessed we were! God is so good!

Suddenly, into this exhilarating atmosphere the phone rang. "Could I speak to Mr. Neufeld?" Doreen echoed back to me in a low, intense voice.

I took the call, hoping I could quickly complete whatever was needed. Instead, I found myself listening to an angry lawyer.

"I'll sue you!" he shouted. "You're the worst kind of per-son I know. I'll get you in court!"

"Wait a minute. Who are you?" I managed to squeak out.

"Don't you know who I am? I've got the power to make you take back everything you've said."

By then I was really puzzled and intimidated. "But what did I do?"

"You did everything wrong. You cannot accuse me, a

lawyer who runs the best firm in the city, of needing to clean up my act. I've done more for the poor folk than anyone else in this town. Everyone respects the Thornson firm. That letter of yours . . ."

In a flash, the bottom seemed to drop right out from under me. I glanced up and saw my wife and four kids looking anxiously at me, sensing that something was wrong.

"That letter of yours is totally false. And why did you send it to the health department?" His voice was rising. "I'm going to take you to court. I'll make sure you are sued aplenty." And with that he hung up

My good day had been turned to ashes. Could he actually sue me? He obviously had the means. With a heavy heart I helped put the boys to bed and then began to reflect with Doreen on the phone conversation. Somewhat innocently, I had put myself into what seemed like a bear trap. Scrambling through my briefcase, I looked at the letter I had written just a few days earlier on behalf of one of the participants in the center's programs. I could hardly believe that this nameless landlord with only a box number was the prominent lawyer we had heard so much about. This is the text of the letter:

> For several months now I have been concerned about the condition of the house Mrs. Jackson is renting from you. Her phone calls to you never get a reply and neither have the six calls I have made to you. Therefore I am documenting the following, with copies to the City of Hamilton Bylaws Department and the Public Health Department:
> Sept. 1—Mrs. Jackson includes a note in her rental payment, saying the furnace does not work.
> Sept. 15—Mrs. Jackson phones your office, leaving a message with the secretary saying that whenever she turns the basement lights on, she sees sparks coming

out of the box. Could there be some loose wires, she asks? She has had to buy a portable electric heater because the furnace is still not working. However, frequently, the fuse blows.

Sept. 20—Mrs. Jackson tells me of her predicament and I encourage her to phone you again. She phones on the same day, declaring that the furnace is not working.

Oct. 1—She includes a note with her rental payment, again asking to have the furnace fixed.

Oct. 15—There is a continuous leak in the plumbing to her kitchen sink, leaving the cabinet wet. Mrs. Jackson calls your office to inform you of this problem, and again mentions the need to have the furnace repaired. I phone your office on behalf of Mrs. Jackson, but receive no reply.

Oct. 20—With the weather turning cold, she phones me again, because her calls seem to have no results. This time I ring your office and leave a message for you to call me back. In spite of repeated calls and messages, I hear nothing from you.

Oct. 24—With no response, I finally draft this letter, hoping that you will take the responsibility that you have as a landlord.

As Doreen and I shared with one another our feelings of intimidation and powerlessness, her words spoke volumes: "If we, in our comfortable home and with all the resources we have, feel threatened and helpless, imagine how Mrs. Jackson feels."

Several days later Mrs. Jackson excitedly called us: "The heat's back on and he's fixed everything." We never heard another word from the lawyer.

-2-
A Remarkable Imprint

So God created humankind in his image, in the image of God he created them; male and female he created them. *(Genesis 1:27)*

This is the great mystery of our faith. We do not choose God, God chooses us. From all eternity we are hidden "in the shadow of God's hand" and "engraved on his palm." Before any human being touches us, God "forms us in secret" and "textures us" in the depth of the earth, and before any human being decides about us, God "knits us together in our mother's womb."[4] *—Henri J. M. Nouwen*

We may not have a lot of money to share and things, but we have a lot of love to share. "Good News" is being able to say to myself that I have something good and that is that I care about people and help them. *—North Ender living below the poverty line*

Lavish Generosity

"Jason and Pam are on the phone," I called out to Doreen. "They're asking us to drop by their house tonight. They have a surprise for us, and they won't say anything more."

We both agreed that this was an invitation we couldn't refuse. We were learning to be more flexible with our schedules and planning. North Enders are spontaneous and generally do not make plans weeks in advance. Soon we were on our way, with not much of a clue as to what to expect.

Pam occasionally worked outside the home, usually in part-time, minimum-wage situations with the fast-food industry. Homemaking was a gift she cherished and made good use of. It was very important for their family to offer hospitality to people of all backgrounds and cultures.

Complementing Pam was her husband, Jason, who was the enthusiastic fix-up man around the house. He had been employed most of his life in a large factory that made brand-name soaps and cosmetics. The business had been purchased recently by a company from the United States that then down-sized and laid off many of the older workers. Jason had fallen victim to this increasingly common trend. Unjustly, very little company pension came from his years of work. When his unemployment insurance ran out, Jason and Pam reluctantly applied for public assistance. It would still be several years before they would be able to receive their modest old-age government security pensions.

This delightful and good-natured couple showed compassion to those who were suffering. Indeed, in their own home they loving cared for their thirty-year-old daughter, Brenda, who had a severe developmental disability and was unable to function in a school setting. Not until a few years earlier had space in a specialized day program become available to her, where she received individual care.

Pam and Jason had discovered the center only a few years before and were a pleasure to have around. Despite challenges at home that consumed so much of their time and despite their lack of material resources, they took an optimistic view of life. Whenever possible they participated in the programs and volunteered with the children's activities.

We entered their small, older home and were given a relaxed welcome, so rare in a busy world. Unfortunately, Jason had not been able to overcome his compulsion to smoke, and the room showed evidence of that. This plus cramped living space and worn furnishings added up to less than the neatness we were accustomed to.

Coffee was already brewing. But before I could take a sip from the steaming cup she handed to me, Pam enthusiastically said, "Guess what? We've received some inheritance money—four thousand dollars! When the money arrived, we both immediately told ourselves, 'Now we have something to give to the center.'"

Opening the envelope that she handed to us, we were taken aback when we saw that the "something" was thirteen one-hundred-dollar bills, just short of one third of their inheritance.

"You can't give that much," we protested. "You could use it yourself. That's a lot more than a 10-percent tithe."

Jason replied, "With the rest of the money we want to get a better stove and some newer furniture. That old couch you're sitting on definitely needs replacing. You know how we like to have people come to our place. But the center also needs our help."

I remembered conducting some interviews for an essay I was writing for a university course. In my survey I asked ten people living on public assistance the question, " If you had an annual income of fifty thousand dollars, how would things change for you?" Six out of the ten immediately talked about contributing to others. As one person put it, "Oh, my God, I can't even think of that. I can't fathom it. I'd just help a lot of other people. I'd be able to help my church, my family, and my friends."

I also thought about an article in one of our church publications that had etched the term "lavish giving" into my faith consciousness. The author had made a point of how we are called to follow the example of God's generosity. So here, in practical terms, this article had come alive for me. Pam and Jason had given, not out of their excess, or even their abundance, but out of the generosity of their hearts and their appreciation of the center.

What they were doing was claiming that original goodness, that initial inheritance, that comes from being designed in God's image. I wondered what we could do with all that we inherit from our Creator if we were to take full ownership of that "estate"?

One of God's Favorite Children

No matter how I looked at her, Lois was not appealing to me. She was heavy—much too heavy. Breast cancer surgery, coupled with inadequate supportive attire, had left her looking quite lopsided. There was a clumsiness about her, and her lack of coordination spilled out everywhere. When Lois walked, it appeared as if she would topple over, but somehow she always managed to get around.

Returning to the center one day after some visits, I stopped in to say hello to the participants in a sewing class. Just at that moment Lois had managed to allow the needle of the sewing machine she was using to go in and out of her index finger. In spite of her pain, she was determined to complete her tailoring project before she would give attention to her injury.

In my view, Lois was often out of touch with reality in terms of what she was able to do. Though she talked a lot and could be eloquent, she tended to overestimate the contributions she could make. Early in life she became prone to epileptic seizures and had been placed in an institution because her low-functioning family could not cope with the illness. The effects of this long-term stay in a mental health facility with few resources meant she didn't experience a normal socialization process.

A remarkable change occurred in Lois after she had begun to participate regularly in the center's programs. Generally, the few paid staff at the center were augmented with five to seven youthful VSers who came from all over the United States and Canada, usually serving for one or two years. They were well liked in the community, with their boundless energy, enthusiasm, willingness to learn, and a faith commitment that manifested itself in practical giving. Through their regular, basic life-skills assistance and friendship with her, Lois had been able to improve her social ability and live on her own. She was always proud to introduce her special VSer[5] to new participants or visitors to the center.

Nevertheless, in groups she often came across as abrasive, especially in the way she would overestimate her abilities. What could one say to a person who was determined to help out with the teenage club program even though she did not have the ability to relate effectively to adolescents? When she looked up at me with those big watery eyes, in such pleading ways, often with her mouth hanging open, I had difficulty knowing how to respond.

On her own, Lois started writing poems to share with her friends at the center. She wasn't a particularly great poet, and at first I paid little attention to her creations. But one day she brought us the following poem:

Jesus Accepts Us

Through trials and errors we come to him
Hoping each day he will forgive our sins.
As I know, Lord, you accept us anyhow
So I come to you and humbly bow.

While serving God, no matter what we say,
Please, God, help us in every way.
Help us to show mercy unto others
As we should be like sisters and brothers.

He accepts us no matter what race or kin we may be;
As God loves us all we can plainly see.
He shows us mercy when things go wrong,
And we end this story by singing a song.

He doesn't reject anyone,
But he waits for us to come to him when we go wrong.
We do this by asking for forgiveness when we pray;
But we should do this in a very kind way.

Jesus, I want to come to you,
Even though my life be lonely and blue.
So dear Lord, I hope you will come to me when I pray,
Not only on Sunday, but every day.

Prayer
Thanks, Heavenly Father, for accepting me
When I pray with all my heart.
I give you thanks at all times for helping me
to become one of your favorite children.

This I pray in your name.
Amen and Amen.[6]

What's this about being one of God's favorite children? My response was indignation. How dare she make such a claim?

I thought again, more deeply, and perhaps more theologically, and realized how precious her statement was. It was my own bias that had made me react. Was not God's remarkable imprint present in all human beings? Did God not create each one of us in God's image? In God's eyes are we not *all* God's favorite children? With such common roots, regardless of oppression or personal brokenness, how dare we underestimate even one of God's people? How wonderful that Lois could feel that special affirmation from God. I had to learn to give her the applause she deserved.

Twenty-five Cents a Hug

The overwhelming task that faced the ever-expanding center and emerging faith community was enlarging the facility. The center had moved several times, from a storefront to a large house with a walkout basement and finally to an empty church facility in the same neighborhood. Along with the dream of a building complex with lots of space came an urgency to make it accessible for persons with physical disabilities.

We had to call on the strongest men available to carry those in a wheelchair up the narrow, half-story stairway leading to the main room. The stairs were too confined to allow anyone to help from the sides, so even the huskiest were intimidated by the strains of the task. Most male VSers could write home about this challenging role, especially when the person they were carrying was heavier than they were. The projected cost to make the building accessible was a minimum of 200,000 dollars. For a small church and social ministry, this was a major undertaking.

To complicate matters, three-quarters of the congregation lived on disability, unemployment insurance, student loans, or some other form of government assistance. There was not one wealthy person in the mix. To put it realistically, the church had no money for expansion, and the center was always struggling to keep up with programming needs. But there was keen vision, plenty of enthusiasm, and most of all, a community that didn't want to give up on the dream of a more adequate, accessible building.

It was in this small congregation of broken but loving, energetic people that the vision began to move toward reality. One Sunday morning after the worship service had already begun, a welcomer announced that Julia had arrived in her wheelchair and needed to be carried up the stairs. Volunteers quickly came forward while the spirited singing of "Jesus Is a Friend" continued.

As Julia entered the sanctuary, to everyone's surprise she got out of her wheelchair, stood somewhat awkwardly, and slowly walked halfway down the center aisle. Grabbing onto a chair but still standing, she asked to make an announcement. We were used to impromptu sharing, so shouts of "Go ahead, Julia" and "Tell us what you have" rose from the congregation.

"Well, there's two things I want to say to you. As you can see, I'm walking again. Thank you, God, for taking care of me!

"But just as important, I want you all to know that I have faith that we will raise all the money we need. It's time we fix up this building so people like me can come in with our wheelchairs and scooters and canes. I'm starting a fundraiser."

Pointing to her wheelchair parked in the back of the church, we all noticed a sign that read, "Twenty-five Cents a Hug. Support the Welcome Inn Building Fund."

Yes, I was a little cynical. Who'd give a quarter to hug someone in a wheelchair?

Yet in a short while Julia had raised well over two hundred dollars. When she went to the public assistance office, social workers couldn't resist her contagious joyful spirit. They readily made contributions, sometimes emptying their wallets and purses of not only quarters, but also the occasional loonie (the Canadian dollar coin). All received their hugs. Julia's participation in City Hall events put her in touch with a number of politicians, including the mayor. They not only gave to the cause but also became aware of the work of Welcome Inn.

When the mayor came to the official opening of the renovated building he already knew much about the center.

Julia's gift to the center went even further. Her friendly, optimistic spirit ignited a number of exciting fundraisers that helped bring the red line in the thermometer chart to its full height. The first-ever walkathon around the North End brought many people out who not only raised a significant amount of money but also gained a new appreciation for the beauty of the neighborhood. Newspapers covered the story and highlighted the significance of the architecture of many of the older buildings instead of focusing on the usual negative aspects. With the waterfront on two sides of the North End, the possibilities of a park at the bay front began to get some positive attention.

Julia's gifts from the Creator were being multiplied. To replace the forms of negativity that had infiltrated the inner city, a beautiful tapestry was being woven.

Hey, Mister, Are You Up in Heaven?

I noticed one evening that the eave trough over the center's entrance was blocked with leaves. I was tired of being pelted with drops of water, so I retrieved the center's extension ladder and quickly made it to the second rung from top, where I could just barely reach up and clear the blockage.

While I was up there, I heard a sound below. It was one of the neighborhood boys, perhaps nine years old, whom I'd seen several times, playing around the center. He had never come to any of our kids' programs. He seemed kind of lost, and I wondered what his home situation was like. Couldn't his parents have at least replaced that tattered, green T-shirt that hung over his stooped, skinny shoulders? Why were his worn-out runners two sizes too big? Didn't he have friends to play with? Why was he always alone, wandering around at night, with no supervision?

I had been too busy to pay much attention to him. Whenever he came anywhere close to me, I brushed him off, but later felt guilty that I hadn't heeded him. There was perhaps a reason for my inadequate response, but to be sure, not a good reason.

My mind was on the recent vandalism in the area. At the adjacent school some "proud" North End kids had spray-painted on the bricks in bold letters, "The North End Lives." I wondered if it was meant to be negative, or did it have something to do with an identity that could, in fact, be positive?

Broken windows at the center bore evidence of frustrated youth without enough to do. I needed to get to the underlying reason why individuals would damage a building that housed programs for their benefit.

Yet the willful destruction bothered me, and sometimes my anger would filter out in unhelpful ways. I was in such a frame of mind when I'd seen the lonely boy in the backyard and yelled at him to get out of there or I'd call the police.

But on this occasion, as I stood precariously on the penultimate rung of the ladder, the boy seemed to know he was safe from any "no trespassing" harassment. We eyed each other as he looked straight up at me. Then in a shrill but sincere way, he asked, "Hey, mister, are you up in heaven?"

For a moment I was startled and almost fell off the ladder. An answer didn't seem readily available to me. But finally I said, "Well, not exactly, but there is a heaven, and it's just a bit farther up." I paused. "But wait a minute. There's a heaven right here as well."

"What do you mean? Things are pretty rough for me. Nobody likes me."

"Not even your parents?"

With that invitation, my nameless new friend poured out the frustrations of his home setting. He painted a picture of unemployed parents who drank heavily, argued aggressively, and often kicked him out into the streets.

He continued, "We never have much food in the house, so every once in a while my mom takes me to the shelter where I get a good meal. I know she loves me; my dad, too. But why can't they always be good? I want a home like everyone else. I got to go."

And with that he vanished. I was still hanging onto the eave trough with one hand, ready to finish my "heavenly" job.

The words, "Hey, mister, are you up in heaven?" captivated my thoughts over the next while. After all, my new friend could have simply and sincerely asked me, "Where is heaven?"

It was clear to me that he wasn't experiencing much of God's reign in his home setting. Did he have a notion of golden streets out there, where life would be pleasant in the great by-and-by, without the painful worries he encountered? Much more likely, he longed for some of that good life to get to him right now.

I was ashamed for the way I had earlier chased him from our backyard. It dawned on me that when someone hangs around at the center and breaks a window, I can respond in two ways: I can buy into the negativity and see an undisciplined, unruly young punk deliberately damaging our property, and through my angry reaction actually match the destructive behavior of the youth. Or I can view the person as someone who has been fashioned by God with enormous potential and who may be mucking up his life, but nonetheless has good qualities that can be brought to the surface. I wondered what the possibilities might have been if I'd responded to him with the latter attitude.

Fortunately, a new opportunity to put this attitude into practice had emerged in a most unlikely place. Had my presence up on the ladder touched this unhappy young lad with some heavenly goodness? I like to think so. However, I still longed and prayed for a further follow-up meeting in which I could learn his name and begin to help unfold some of that God-given potential.

We'll Take Care of You, Dad

Cynthia and Andrew, along with their son, Peter, who had a developmental disability, lived in one of the older buildings in the North End. Some of Andrew's more well-to-do siblings had good jobs and expensive homes in other parts of the city. But it was this family, living well below the poverty line, who took George, Andrew's aged, bedridden father, into their tiny home and lovingly looked after him for more than ten years.

During those years, George's other children rarely came to see him; they seemed to have abandoned him for the upwardly mobile life. Andrew and Cynthia graciously gave him a central place in their small, cluttered living space. There were no extra bedrooms, so the dining and living rooms became the palliative care suite. Before the public health nurse began coming on a regular basis, it was Andrew who carried his father to the washroom, bathed him regularly, and made sure his sheets were clean.

It had not been easy to convert their house into a nursing home, but George had a stubborn streak and refused to go into an institution. In spite of his dad's weaknesses and alienation from the rest of the family, Andrew knew that George needed the honor and care that every father deserves from a son. When George died at home at the age of eighty-two, I was privileged to say these words at the funeral service:

A Service of Celebration for George Harkman

Friends and family, we are grieving the death of George Harkman, who died peacefully on December 22. After major illnesses he eventually was confined to a bed in the living room of Andrew, his son, Cynthia, his daughter-in-law, and Peter, his grandson, where he received loving care for over ten years. God honors such consistent, long-term caring, knowing that you sacrificed your living-room space, your time, and your resources to demonstrate love. From his bed George could see how you decorated the Christmas tree and carefully included him in the already wrapped presents under the tree. Although it had been tough to find something that George in his condition could appreciate, you did your best, and now hoped to be able to spend at least one more Christmas with him.

But God had a different plan. God called him out of this life as he will call every one of us someday. Today we are reminded again that our lives on this earth are temporary. Dwight L. Moody once said, "Let God have your life. He can do more with it than you can do." God has crafted all of us in God's image, giving us the breath of being. We must claim that God-given quality and allow it to flourish.

The last years were difficult for George, being totally immobilized. He did, however, enjoy the things in his presence, such as the morning sunlight brightening up his darkened room on the south side of the little house. Often he would point to the bright budgies in the cage that hung right beside his bed. "They've been singing songs just for me all morning," he would say.

Some of you had the opportunity of knowing George while he was still healthy. I'm told he used to love tinkering around with cars. It's a blessing to have good health, and sometimes we take it for granted. Perhaps we need to be reminded that "all good gifts come from above," and that God, through God's grace, gives us the ability to walk and enjoy the healthy functions of our bodies.

George knew it wouldn't be long until his death. Occasionally he would say he wanted to die. As I visited him, I sometimes wondered what his thoughts were about the future. One thing I can say is that toward his last days he began appreciating prayer more and more, and sometimes he would indicate how often God was on his mind. Instead of being depressed and discouraged about his physical condition, he would look up at me and say in his typical way, "Okay then."

In looking back now, we are thankful for our last visit with George. That Monday evening just before his death, sixteen of us from the Welcome Inn Church came to sing Christmas carols for him. We all crowded around his bed, and in the tightly packed room, the music that came forth was overwhelming and life-giving. George was deeply touched, and some of us can still hear him softly uttering the words to "Silent Night." The simple song "Jesus loves me this I know" brought tears to his eyes. We remember how at one point he straightened himself out, tried to lift his head, and smiled. Then he looked directly into the eyes of Rachel, one and a half years old, the youngest member of our group, a moment of joy for him. Although he couldn't really eat all the grapes the VSers had brought, he tasted one. Perhaps he could claim it as his final Communion and Eucharist feast.

In the last hours of his life he called for Peter,

which I believe was a sign of his caring for his grand-son. He also spoke two words to Andrew and Cynthia, "I'm sorry," which was his way of leaving things right with the people who were his kin and had cared for him so lovingly all these years. Marietta, George's granddaughter, told me that very recently she had sung "Amazing Grace" for him, which had touched him greatly.

We want to praise God for George's life. God knew him and knows him and has taken him to his home. When Jesus calls, whether it be in our final hours on this earth or whether it be for a task right here in our daily lives, let us be ready. May God help us. Amen.

Reflections on a Wordless Poem

"This is for you, *mm*, for you, *mmm*. Here, take it, *mm*, take it, especially, *mmm*, for you."

I could barely make out the words, which were punctuated with this "mm" sound so characteristic of Barbara. In her hand, she clutched what looked like a piece of scrap paper, a big grin on her face. As I turned it over, I saw it was full of a mixture of continuous *e*'s and *u*'s (or were they inverted *m*'s?) written across every line, with no empty spaces. A more careful look revealed breaks in this unusual script, clearly suggesting long and short words, a neat collage of expressions that would speak nothing to intellectually stimulated and focused minds.

I graciously accepted this wordless poem and told Barbara I would read it when I got home. She gave me the widest smile imaginable and then meandered out to the van that was waiting to take her home.

Barbara was one of our special friends who we regularly picked up from a lodging home and brought to church. While driving the van for a few months, I used to play a created-on-the-spot game with her. It started when I challenged her one day to tell me the color of the traffic light in front of us. "It's r-r-r-r-red," she would say, but by the time she'd finished her sentence the light had turned green. After that I would frequently tease her, making sure the question was perfectly timed to coincide with the change in lights. Her radiant smile told me she enjoyed every minute of the jesting.

Barbara had little money or resources and had no known relatives. A while back she had ended up in a semi-nursing home situation in which the owner was profiting excessively from housing a number of people with disabilities. Staff worked at minimum wage, and the level of care could be rated only as minimal. On one occasion one of our volunteers was so frustrated with the unwashed clothing that Barbara regularly wore that she went over and laundered Barbara's entire wardrobe. Needless to say, the personnel at the home were very embarrassed.

I noticed that the more attention I paid her, the more I could recognize words here and there. What became clear was that she loved people, cherished relationships, and desperately wanted to communicate.

In the course of all my activities, I almost forgot about the poem tucked into a folder in my briefcase. But a few days later it fell out, and there it was, lying in front of me on my desk. I must read this, I guiltily thought to myself. Didn't I promise to examine the wordless poem?

First of all, the writing showed purposefulness. There was nothing haphazard about it, as one might conclude on first glance. Barbara had deliberately set out to craft a letter, and because she had so much to say, she filled every space. There was nothing that she wanted to hide from me. I'd like to think that she wholeheartedly gave me a complete and honest treatise of some of her deepest feelings. She began on one corner of the page—I'm not even sure which corner—and then intentionally worked through the spaces until every cavity was filled.

I still have the poem in one of our scrapbooks. Can I learn something more from this dedicated, purposeful communicating?

There is a sense of order in it. While some of the *e*'s and *u*'s run over the lines, it never distracts from the overall congruity. In the poem, Barbara had displayed a consistency so often lacking in her life. Good-hearted folks might have paid attention to her at Christmastime by showering her with gifts, but she was ignored the rest of the year. She may have gotten into a sheltered workshop for a few hours each day, but the rest of the day, on holidays, and on weekends, seldom was anyone there for her.

Barbara was also very resourceful. The letter in front of me is a recycled piece with a recipe scribbled on the back. Where she got it, I don't know, but it certainly had been put to good use. It reminds me of what I've seen over and over: that people living in poverty and driven by necessity creatively make do.

Most important, I think the letter conveys a desire to contribute. In our work-oriented society, where much of our identity is shaped by our employment, people crafted by God who are unable to compete inevitably receive a jolt to their identity. Warehousing people in substandard lodging homes and providing them few possibilities to contribute leaves a portion of our society primarily in the category of recipients. Indeed, we have labeled them based on what they cannot do, rather than on what they can do. Barbara's letter calls on a work-driven society to alter social structures and allow even someone like her a "just day's wages" for her contributions.

There may be other wordless poetry that are not in circulation, perhaps hidden away in a briefcase or carelessly tossed into a waste bin. Such precious material awaits discovery.

I Am the One

The center was expanding rapidly. More and more programs were being generated as people from the community brought us their needs and their vision. As codirectors, Doreen and I, together with some others, crafted a directional statement:

> Since God has created all people in God's image, therefore every individual, regardless of background, education, experience, culture, income level, and status in society, has something positive to contribute. The mutual recognition of strengths in one another through relationships fosters a giving and receiving exchange. Thus the Welcome Inn becomes not a handout agency, where traffic flows one way. Rather, a forum is developed where good qualities of one's life can be shared, including the important Christian faith, as one is open to also accept the positive aspects of others. Everyone is important at the Welcome Inn. Everyone has worth.[7]

These words served as a reminder that was needed in a climate where the rush to do good for others often superseded listening to see what a person in need might contribute. Several of our volunteers had somewhat naively begun an evening youth program without consultation with the community. There was no problem getting the young people to come. But the invitation to drop in for an evening of fun had brought in so many that they took over the building. In desperation, the intimidated volunteers called the police, who then sent everyone home. This overly aggressive, authoritarian approach had exacerbated the frustrations of the youth, who on subsequent evenings increased vandalism around the center.

Good intentions had destroyed the potential of a positive experience for the youth. Later parents gave comments like, "I could have told you what would happen." "Why didn't you talk to us ahead of time?" "Some of us would have helped you out."

I pondered such experiences as I rode my bike through the North End neighborhood. By then I recognized people on almost every street, and I had learned the value of stopping to chat. North Enders had lots of time, but they often judged that I did not. My own busyness gained me the distinctive nickname (perhaps not so distinctive) of Hugo the Go-Go. On this particular evening I was considering how we needed to consult more with people who benefited from the programs, but I couldn't come up with many practical ways to do that.

The next day I received a call from a single mom who said that her thirteen-year-old daughter, Shelly, had written a poem she wanted to share with us. "Remember our discussion a few days ago on how service needs to be a two-way street? This may help us," she proudly explained. Shelly's poem was simple, but profound.

I Am the One

I am the one who helps;
  I am the one who needs help.

I am the one who cares;
  I am the one who needs care.

I am the one who listens;
  I am the one who needs listening too.

I am the one who does things for others;
  I am the one who needs things done for me.
  Please help![8]

Clearly, the help she was requesting in the concluding line was not the one-way kind of help so characteristic of the charity model. Teenagers of every economic group want to get in on designing activities of which they can be a part. They instinctively know that everyone has a remarkable imprint attributed to a God who created us in God's image.

When the conference of supporting churches gathered a few weeks later, it was not the center's directional statement that caught their imagination. Rather, it was Shelly's poem. I concluded that maybe it should be so.

-3-

Standing on Common Ground

The rich and the poor meet together; The LORD is the Maker of them all. *(Proverbs 22:2, KJV)*

Rich people need the poor. Without contact with them they run the danger of feeling completely self-sufficient, of not needing anyone, of feeling completely secure in their knowledge and power.

The poor tend to disturb the rich in their false security. And if rich people let themselves be disturbed, then the miracle can happen!
The poor can penetrate through the bars of their prison. The eyes of the poor can seep into their hearts and waken them to new life.
Through a real meeting of the two, the rich can experience that they really have a heart. Their own hearts begin to vibrate and to love.
They also discover their own fears, barriers and search for comfort and security.[9] *—Jean Vanier*

We've Come for the Picnic

"We can't take Mrs. Bea and her three children to our family outing. She's drunk and needs to go home," one of our volunteers explained to me.

It was a beautiful, sunny day. About seventy of us were gathered at the center, waiting for the signal to get into cars. Mothers with children who were laughing and dancing around, men who loved to help with outdoor activities, single folk who cherished intergenerational relationships, people from our supporting congregation, and enthusiastic staff were all eager to spend the day together. It was good to see a number of people join us who represented nationalities and cultures newer to the North End. Many had walked or taken public transportation to participate in this social event geared to family households of all sizes and configurations. We were to be on our way to Hidden Valley for our annual corn roast.

"She's over there," one of the drivers said, pointing her out to me.

Mrs. Bea, a single mom new to our programs, was sitting on the steps to the center holding a grocery bag with wieners and buns. (Participants brought part of the communal meal, while the Welcome Inn supplied corn-on-the-cob, drinks, and desserts.) Her three young children tugged at her side, showing their attachment to her as well as their insecurity in the presence of so many strangers. At the same time, I saw their excitement as they looked forward to this new adventure.

But my heart was heavy. I could tell she had been drinking. We had a policy not to include people in our activities who were under the influence of drugs or alcohol. With slurred speech, she insisted, "I've come all this way on the bus. You can't send me home now."

In our role as codirectors, Doreen and I encouraged staff and volunteers not to pre-judge but to treat people in new and fresh ways. Even when previous behavior showed some negativity, respect was always called for. "Everyone has a kernel of positivism that must be discovered," we said. We advised first to greet the problem drinker gently with a listening ear. Only after you've demonstrated hospitality are you in a position to decline including them in the program.

But now I felt sorry for the three kids, huddled together on the stairs. Should we circumvent our principles and quietly take the whole family in our car? But I knew the staff was pretty much united in honoring our "disqualification" policy.

By now the crowd of mostly regular family-outing goers became aware of our dilemma and began making suggestions. "I can't take her along in my car," one volunteer driver declared. Another firmly stated, "She can come next time, when she's in better shape. Let's be on our way." Others thought that, because she was new, maybe we could take her along.

Finally, one of the women who had conquered some of her addictions through the center's help insisted, "Look, where would I be if the Welcome Inn had not accepted me? They've got nothing to go home to right now. There is no question in my mind. Why not take them all? I'll look after the mom, while some of you adopt the children. I know how to handle drunk people."

With that pronouncement I knew we would have to forget our policy, although I still had mixed feelings about what was best. Several of the staff seemed perturbed, which bothered me, because I'm one who likes unity.

Finally we were on our way. With Mrs. Bea properly chaperoned, no conflicts arose and everyone enjoyed the outing.

However, at our staff meeting several days later, Doreen and I had to face colleagues who questioned our decision. During the discussion, we recognized that we had not paid enough attention to their uneasiness about inconsistency in enforcing the intoxication rule. We also acknowledged that we could have consulted with them more directly. It had been a difficult decision, and we admitted that there was more than one valid approach that could have been taken.

In the course of our two-hour meeting, one of the new staff hired from the neighborhood pointed out how the family outing group brought together people of vastly different economic situations. "Did you know that there are words of wisdom in the Bible that say exactly what you are suggesting?" Doreen responded. "I've found the words from Proverbs very affirming for what is happening in our setting: 'The rich and the poor meet together; the Lord is the Maker of them all.' "

Another staff member added, "It clearly sounds like we are mandated by our Creator, who gave life to all people, to foster situations where persons with different economic means actually form relationships and learn to appreciate one another. The writer assumes we will meet together because we have been made by the Lord."

Our stimulating discernment moved to identifying some of the societal structures that fly in direct opposition to what this "script from the Scriptures" had to say to us. We all agreed that there was a problem when city policy grouped those who are poor into housing complexes like the Survey, while expensive homes were built in wealthy parts of the city. As we talked, we found affirmation for the steps the center was taking in bringing together people from different social classes for an outing by the waterfront.

"This is countercultural, like Jesus was," one VSer said.

"But we can't bring people who are intoxicated," another staff member responded.

I recalled a lecture by Mary Jo Leddy and recounted some of her points to the group.[10] Leddy had carefully examined what she called "the bondage" found in both the rich and the poor. Those who are poor know that liberation from an unhealthy system that seems to trap people in poverty is necessary. That is their bondage. For the rich the bondage has to do with our consumer culture and often plays itself out through stress, anxiety, addictions, and broken relationships. Her final words have continued to stick with me: "Let the middle class cast off their invisible chains. Let the poor break their most visible chains. And let them hold hands together."

Our mostly middle-class staff began to seriously examine ourselves. We identified on the chalkboard addictions to certain food and drink; a preoccupation with schedules and structure; a fixation on consumerism and productivity; how we relish competition, and not just in sports and table games. It soon dawned on us that if we followed our "exclusionary" policy in a consistent way, perhaps some of us would not be permitted to go on that family outing.

It became clear that we also had our addictions and needed others to walk with us and guide us to more healthy levels of functioning. What beauty there is when people from all walks of life, sharing a common goodness, take the opportunity to meet together. When we are in proximity to one another and support each other in our brokenness, we celebrate our combined strengths.

Yes, I Can Walk

As a child I romanticized the healing stories of Jesus and particularly loved the one in which Jesus healed the man who had been lowered through the roof by his friends (Mark 2:1-12). But as I became older, with my rational mind developing, I became a little skeptical that God could actually physically heal someone in this day and age.

I was in the office awaiting the arrival of one of the VSers for a supervision session when the phone rang. It was Steve, a painting contractor, whom we had first met after he was released from jail. He had served time for a series of break-ins, including some bank robberies. "I'm stopping by the center in twenty minutes to pick you up," he said. "You've got to come, and bring one of your volunteers with you. We're going to take this elderly lady, Jane, out for a ride. I've been hired to paint the outside of her house, and she told me she hasn't been out of her house in seven years."

How could I refuse? If Steve could delay his painting job, surely the supervision session could wait.

"Okay, Steve. I'll bring one of the VSers with me and we'll try to be ready when you get here." I was thinking a VS supervision session that included a man who not long before had walked into a bank with a sawed-off shotgun and demanded money might be quite interesting for the supervisor as well as the VSer.

Jane was in a wheelchair and barely able to maneuver to

the front door to answer Steve's persistent knocking. Sure enough, we discovered a woman who had been isolated in her home since her husband died more than seven years earlier. Her children had long ago left home and seemingly didn't pay much attention to her. The house, though neatly kept, was dark and dingy. Jane lacked the energy even to open the blinds. Her world had begun to close in on her. She felt abandoned, with little to live for. When she refused to accept our offer of an afternoon outing, I was ready to give up. But Steve insisted that she try it this one time: "Do you remember the botanical gardens and the flowers you used to enjoy? We'll take you to them. What about driving to the top of the escarpment that overlooks the city? Jane, you have some friends here from Welcome Inn, who love to help people."

Finally, she gave us a weak yes. We pushed her in the wheelchair to the van and managed to get her into the front passenger seat. We wanted her to see as much as possible. It took awhile, but gradually she began to relax and enjoy the ride.

Jane pointed out the changes around town. "There never used to be a gas station there." "When was that building torn down?"

She almost ecstatically enjoyed the soft ice cream we offered her. She'd never had it before. From that timid smile, I witnessed a transformation; her pessimism peeled away and a positive disposition emerged.

When we brought her home, Jane insisted we take a picture of her in front of the house, not in her wheelchair but standing on her own two feet. She was confident and free, with only one hand on the railing. Jane had experienced a measure of healing in her life, including a straightening of her weak, limp legs.

The outing was a turning point for her. Afterward she took the initiative to call an old friend, who put her in touch with a student nurse. The student agreed to visit Jane weekly. The center arranged for ongoing trips that would take her into other settings.

God's grace and healing came to Jane when an unchurched, tenderhearted contractor whose past included armed robbery, a VSer spending a year in service, and a community center codirector discovered our rich human commonality and spent the afternoon together. Jane experienced a new hope, and the three of us gained a form of healing and holy laughter that couldn't be contained. Back at the center, our souls vibrated with joy, which we shared with all as we recounted the exciting adventure. The supervision session had been successful!

Sharing the Headlines with Artie

As was his custom, Artie was at the center with one of his suggestions. "Hey, Hugo, you've got to come with us on Saturday. There's a march against poverty. You and Doreen and all the VSers need to come."

The longer we lived and ministered in the North End, the more we were convinced of the need to take seriously the voices of those living below the poverty line, who had so much brokenness in their lives.

Artie was born and spent all his thirty-five years in the North End. He had developmental difficulties and had never functioned in a school setting. With little to do with his time, he found friendship at the center and participated in almost every program he was allowed into. Artie had a mischievous smile and an eager disposition, and he would often sit on a bench under the tall evergreen tree by the entranceway, welcoming new people as the unofficial greeter.

Doreen and I were aware of the Poverty Walk, which was organized by a coalition of community agencies, socially minded churches, labor unions, and various peripheral political and social parties. It included some aggressive activists who, in my opinion, were using tactics that didn't fit a nonviolence stance. We had never participated in a protest walk before and were somewhat uncomfortable with it. Some people in our supporting churches and organizations would have stayed miles away from something like this. The idea of joining a group in which some had motivations different from ours didn't sit well with us either.

On the other hand, in our walk with those who were poor, the concern for justice had become increasingly important to us. Advocating for better access to the resources our country provided was part of our calling. By then we were passionate in calling for changes to social systems so that people could more easily break the poverty cycle. What particularly caused our anger to swell was the immediate reduction of social benefits to those who tried to get ahead by earning a few dollars. We also realized that the public assistance rates, which were already far below the poverty line, were actually going down when accounting for inflation. Opportunities to improve the situation were difficult to access for most of the people we knew. Every day we interacted with people who had to fend for basic food and shelter.

But what were we to do? Artie, who himself was on disability and always ran short at the end of the month, was calling on us to join him. Was this a situation in which the rich and poor should meet together?

My discussion with a Quaker friend persuaded me that I could legitimately join others of all kinds of persuasions. "We are united on the basic message we want to communicate," he said. "So I join to help out with the cause, while at the same time I share my reasons for working with justice issues."

Artie was overjoyed when we agreed, though somewhat reluctantly, to accompany him and also to invite others. With the support of one of our VSers, who was strong on social action, we soon had a group of about a dozen promising to go. About half of them were on public assistance.

This event was part of a weeklong awareness and protest action that would eventually end up at the legislative buildings in Toronto. Signatures of support to improve the welfare system would be taken along the way and would be presented to the appropriate politicians. The protest was organized in such a way that people could join for a day or two while a consistent core group would be part of the total event.

The Saturday walk through Hamilton was peaceful and celebrative. Hundreds of people of all ages and economic means mingled freely with one another. Our fears of what others driving by would think vanished completely. This powerful intergenerational experience carried the proclamation of Christ's "good news to the poor" (Luke 4:18).

We listened to various stories along the way. "I'm on this walk for my family and myself," said Jean. "It hurts so much to be looked down on because you are on welfare. I can't help that I was injured in an accident. We're fighting to change things, so we can live like people. It's got to get better."

Mabel shared her frustrations: "So many government forms, so much red tape. Every time you need something you have to go downtown to their offices, where they look at you like you're an animal. That's the feeling I get sometimes."

"The well-off don't know what we are going through," David told us. "The publicity on the poor is always put negatively. It makes me feel like I shouldn't have applied for welfare, even though I need it desperately."

Colleen, a university student with two children, expressed appreciation for the student loans and social assistance she'd received. She was confident she would eventually get off public assistance. But she faced many disappointments, which she shared with us. "My kids come home from school crying sometimes, because the other kids call them welfare bums. We live with that stigma and it's almost impossible to get away from it while you are getting help. Being poor is demeaning; it's always rubbed in. Our welfare system definitely needs to be improved."

As the day continued in perfect weather, people with jobs and those without them fostered new friendships. A common cause of justice had brought us together. Those with easy access to material resources interacted with those who had little. And it was great fun to be together.

"You're glad you came, aren't you?" Artie piped up, giving me a smile that indicated he was pleased at his success in getting me there.

I replied to him and the small group I was walking with, "Whenever the rich and the poor walk together, there is joy in heaven, and on earth."

To my consternation, the next day's paper took up nearly a quarter page with a photo of Artie in his referee shirt and me carrying my jacket in my arms, heading up an endless group of people. (Artie had made sure that the two of us got right in front of the line.) Above our heads, on a banner directly behind us, in large bold print, were the words, "March against Poverty," and in smaller letters, "We refuse to starve in silence."

I was dismayed by the coverage because, while I wanted my immediate community to know I was walking in solidarity with them, I was unprepared for the publicity. I preferred to work quietly in the background. Also, the concern that some people from our supporting churches might not understand tugged at my emotions. One thing was clear. Walking on common ground had put us on the map. Maybe that wasn't so bad after all. I was now forging into an expanded ministry and could no longer remain silent on the many issues around poverty.

Justice in the School

The local school board and the provincial government had acknowledged that schools in older urban neighborhoods often became second-rate, so they had put extra money into the educational facilities in the North End. Our four sons attended these schools, and we were impressed with the high quality of the teaching staff and the modern facilities that had been built during urban renewal.

So it was something of a shock when I received a frantic phone call from Monica, one of the mothers who attended a women's group at the center. "Can we meet at the Welcome Inn? We have a principal who is violent!"

"Tell me more."

"We've got to get Mr. Palmer out of there. He's been grabbing kids and pushing them against the brick wall. More than once he's slapped Darren, and he's got the marks to prove it."

I had heard rumors about this principal's methods of disciplining rowdy kids, but I hadn't taken them too seriously. Our boys did well academically and had never complained about the principal.

The center had an excellent relationship with the schools in the area and often received referrals, especially for tutoring or to one of our youth programs. I enjoyed getting into the classrooms once in a while; on one occasion I had the joyful task of playing Santa Claus to a group of first-graders. At least once a year we invited all the teachers for a luncheon to talk

about how we could be mutually supportive. The school occasionally allowed us to use some of their space for our programs
too. I didn't want to jeopardize such a spirit of cooperation.

Monica continued. "There's four of us parents who have concerns. Will you meet with us? We've already alerted Child
Protection and they will come to the meeting if we can arrange it."

I had mixed feelings about hosting the group, especially if
the Child Protection agency was present, which would make
the meeting official and potentially much more threatening to
the principal. I was troubled that the meeting might be seen as
working against the principal, which could affect how my children were treated at school.

When I suggested that the group meet with the principal
alone, Monica responded, "He's not going to listen to us."

Working toward justice had become very important to me.
The biblical words of Amos resonated in my awareness: "Let
justice roll down like waters, and righteousness like an ever-
flowing stream" (Amos 5:24). But how could justice be
unleashed like a smooth stream (perhaps not so smooth) in
such a volatile situation?

Finally, I agreed to meet with the women at the center.

What I discovered were four extremely upset moms.
Monica, who had taken a social action course, saw this as an
opportunity to aggressively pursue a cause that affected her
own child. Pent-up emotions from her troubled past played
into the anger she was feeling. Two of the other parents each
had a youngster who had difficulty in the classroom. As I listened, I could hear genuine concern beneath the accusations.

With the Child Protection worker's support, the parents
and I met with the principal. Unfortunately, it did not go well.
After we all sat down in Mr. Palmer's office, Monica's first
words were, "I want you out of here." There followed a bar-
rage of accusations, and nothing I said could calm the situation. Mr. Palmer quickly lost his cool too. He denied wrong-

doing and eventually ushered us out of his office. Everyone left frustrated, totally unsatisfied, and with much unfinished business.

I wondered how I could be a Christian presence in the situation. Was there any common ground between this disconcerted group of women and myself? Was there enough evidence pointing toward a problematic principal? What could move us toward a solution?

Only a few days later, I heard another report about kids at the school being "tackled" by Mr. Palmer. This time it came from a youngster new to the school. Now more parents were worried, and something had to be done.

I called the principal, but he wouldn't meet with us. I didn't want to bypass him, but by that time I had no choice but to call the school board. The board director invited me and the parents to a meeting. At first he defended the principal, but as he listened more carefully to our concerns, he admitted that there was a problem and said he would talk with Mr. Palmer.

Somewhere in the course of our conversation the director inadvertently disclosed that Mr. Palmer had a severe form of cancer, which could have explained some of his aggressive behavior. Suddenly our delegation became a little quieter. We felt a measure of compassion and wondered if Mr. Palmer hadn't received help with his frustrations, both personally and in the school context. At the same time we expected but no longer demanded that the school board do something. The director assured us that he also would not tolerate the kind of behavior we had described. He promised to investigate and make sure Mr. Palmer received the right kind of help.

Back at the center, we all agreed it had been a good meeting. We had voiced our frustrations and were confident that corrective action would be taken. It occurred to us that we might do something constructive. We decided to write a letter of support to Mr. Palmer, with an offer to help set up a parents group to assist with problematic students and to help the school in other ways.

We never heard another complaint about Mr. Palmer mishandling kids. Several months later, he died at the age of fifty-three, and it was the newly organized parents group, including Monica and her friends, who served refreshments at the memorial service at the school.

The Jack Davies Center

Just a few doors down from the original center was a two-story brick building with a storefront on the first floor and a residence on the second. It was one of those old-fashioned, inner-city stores that clashes with the modern shopping mall phenomenon edging into the area. By the time we arrived in the North End, only a few were left, most with vacant lots adjacent to them.

Jack Davies' store had everything. The old hardwood counter, with its drawers and glassed cabinets, contained screws, washers, bolts, nails, fuses, and every piece of plumbing imaginable. Stacked to the top on shelves were toasters, electric frying pans, dishes, cutlery, and much more. Hanging from the ceiling were lamps, sleighs, large pots, baby bathtubs, car seats, and anything that needed an open space because of its size or shape. The oiled maple floor had only narrow passages for maneuvering between all the basic household supplies stacked around. Anything not housed on the main floor could be found in the basement, which also contained a fix-up center for glass and screen doors plus an appliance repair shop. The entrance was very narrow, with shovels and rakes, garden seeds, cement bags, and trowels all vying for space.

But the most important fixture in the store was Jack Davies himself, who could often be found punching away at the old-fashioned cash register. He was a long-term North Ender who had inherited the store and its contents from his father. Not only did Jack have everything it took to keep a house in shape, but he also had the know-how. People came to him for advice on every imaginable problem. Because Jack was a wise and sociable guy, he had earned a reputation as a listener, counselor, teacher, coach, mentor, and anything else one could conceive of. But he once emphatically told me, "I'm not one of those religious-priest guys." He would leave that up to me.

Every day Hamie, who was developmentally disabled, came to the store, sat on a bag of dog food, and chatted with customers. While Jack was getting Hamie his regular free coffee, Hamie sang out, "Remember, four teaspoons of sugar, heaping." Many customers joined the conversation and stayed awhile.

Frequently, the discussion turned to all the changes in the community having to do with urban renewal. People were bitter about friends and family being forced to sell their homes with little notice and not enough compensation to buy a comparable house in another part of the city. The most difficult part had been seeing the social fabric of the old North End disintegrate, with so many leaving.

"Couldn't there have been more money available for the renewal of existing housing?" Mrs. Burkholder ranted. "Why did they have to destroy so much of our community life?" She lamented that the houses on her street had been well kept and neat, but the government had needed them for what was called the Perimeter Road, which still was not built. "All I see where my house used to stand is an empty lot," she said.

There were many other conversations at Jack's in which neighborhood problems would be sorted out, North End celebrations germinated, and newcomers like me welcomed to the North End. Jack was not connected with any religious group, but he had solid values and principles of living that made him an asset in the community. I began to realize that God was present and at work in this man and in this unofficial center of hope within a changing North End.

I wondered if the Jack Davies Center, as I had somewhat whimsically called it, could be complementary to our center, where we attempted to be a Christian presence. Was there a role in us working together and forming positive relationships? Could we learn from each other? Was my missional task to help Jack identify what in his actions was of God?

For more than a year I often stepped into the store, even if there was nothing I needed to purchase. Other North Enders did the same. Jack would refer people to us, and we would promote his store. Then one day I was saddened to hear that the store had been expropriated and Jack was moving to another part of the city. He thanked me for my help and added, "I know there's a guy upstairs who's taking care of me." A few years later I heard he had died when the small plane he was piloting crashed in a field just outside of Hamilton.

I Have a Bone to Pick: Meeting the Mayor

I grew up feeling intimidated by officials in authority, such as police and politicians. Could it be that my somewhat sheltered Mennonite upbringing had steered me away from meaningful interaction with such people? Or was it simply my lack of confidence that kept me in my comfort zones?

The center had just moved into a larger facility. At a community planning meeting, we discussed who we would invite to the opening celebration, which would include a dedication service and an open house. Christina, a resident of the neighborhood, quickly called out, "Let's invite the mayor. He should be here." So not only did we invite the mayor but as many other government officials as we could think of. We wanted this dedication to be different from a traditional one in which few beyond the church constituency received invitations.

On the day of the opening, people arrived on foot, by car, by bicycle, and by public transportation. I was thrilled by the turnout. A large limousine pulled up and people excitedly called out, "The mayor is here!" As staff leaders of the center, I knew it would be up to me and Doreen, and perhaps the board chair, to welcome him. Doreen and I had made our way to the front lawn with several dozen others, eagerly anticipating the man who would emerge from that long, shiny vehicle, something rarely, if ever, seen in this neighborhood. "Do I call him Mr. Morrow," I wondered, "or do I use the more formal greeting Your Worship?" Something in me strongly resisted the latter. God is the only person I worship.

Precisely at two o'clock, the time set for the celebration to begin, the limo driver opened the doors and Mayor Morrow emerged with his entourage of well-dressed personnel. "Let's invite him in," our board chair whispered to me. "I didn't know he would bring so many bodyguards."

"I guess he's a pretty important man," I thought. Now what was that title again? Before I could move, I heard Russell, an unemployed family man with three growing sons, step out and say, "Hi, Bob, welcome here! You know, I've got a bone to pick with you!"

Another friend quickly added, "What are you going to do about those increases in transit fares? You know it's hurting us people on disability."

Madeline, who was friendly and welcoming no matter what the occasion, quickly added, "This is a great place here. Come on in and join us."

All my nervous images of formality disappeared at that moment when we all stood on common ground. Doreen and I shook hands with Mayor Bob and ushered him into the center for the ceremony. The prophetic words of Mary's Magnificat, "He has brought down the powerful from their thrones, and lifted up the lowly"(Luke 1:52), were being claimed, as was the sacred, ancient directive for the rich and the poor to meet together.

–4–
Making Up a New Card Game

The Spirit of the Lord is upon me, because he has anointed me to bring good news to the poor.
He has sent me to proclaim release to the captives and recovery of sight to the blind, and to let the oppressed go free, to proclaim the year of the Lord's favor. *(Luke 4:18-19)*

When Jesus said, "I have come to bring good news to the poor," he meant that he would give us a spiritual lift; it would make us feel better; it would give us more self-confidence, and it would create a world where there wouldn't be as many rich and as many poor—we would all be equal.
—A North Ender living below the poverty line

True evangelical faith cannot lie dormant.
It clothes the naked,
it feeds the hungry,
it comforts the sorrowful,
it shelters the destitute,
it serves those that harm it,
it binds up that which is wounded,
it has become all things to all people.[11]
—Menno Simons, 1539

A New Card Game

The discussion was intense.

"Our government needs to put more money into mental health programs."

"We need more subsidized housing. It's no wonder the homeless population is increasing in crisis proportions."

"So many people talk about people on public assistance in a negative way."

"I would like to see our politicians live on welfare rates for a month. Then they would have more compassion for the poor."

I was attending a forum with mostly well-to-do-people, who were sitting around tables in a posh lounge in a downtown hotel. The setting seemed entirely out of keeping with the subject of "Hunger in Our City." Most participants were from area service agencies that dealt with the poor, but had no personal relationships with them. This group of educated and well-dressed social workers, teachers, counselors, psychiatrists, and others in the health services were strongly motivated to see changes in the social services, but were frustrated in their efforts.

Renee had been very excited when I asked her if she wanted to accompany me to the meeting. "Yeah, I would love to say something about what it means to live on a disability check. I would like people to see me as normal."

Generally a fun-loving person, Renee had a quiet though intense personality and could be sharply confrontational.

When she was in her early twenties, doctors discovered some major heart problems and placed her on a permanent disability pension.

When we walked through the lavish hotel to the lounge where the meeting was in progress, I felt Renee getting uncomfortable. The discomfort increased as we entered the room of professionals, all actively engaged with one another. She immediately detected that she was the only person in the room living below the poverty line. She knew firsthand the tendency to talk *about* the poor and *for* the poor, rather than *to* them. And I had started to refuse to attend meetings where people talked about those in the lowest economic sector without any of them being present. So I was pleased that Renee was able to attend.

A capable facilitator led the conversation around the tables. After much talk, she began summarizing the many action items. These always seemed to move toward the general, and then didn't say very much.

Renee had been very quiet throughout but, mustering up her courage, she finally spoke. "Maybe we just have to make up a new card game. The old euchre games we've been playing just don't work anymore. We've got to stop having winners and losers, and that can only happen when the wealthy release their purse strings and we become friends with one another."

Renee received a round of applause. After a bit of awkward silence, a small committee was set up to work at some solutions.

From the beginning of the center, the word *client* was never used. Instead of a focus on client and helper, people were simply referred to as "Welcome Inn friends." Our sign outside read, "Meet Your Friends Here." In this way it was felt that the center could complement the professional helping agencies, while at the same time forging new territory in which the old categories of "helper versus helpee" could be broken down.

The theology of Welcome Inn used imagery from the apostle Paul's writings on the body of Christ[12] and was directed toward bringing out the giftedness of all people. There were no pure recipients or pure givers. All were in the circle—families requiring food, youth coming to the soccer club, people participating in programs, VSers, staff, volunteers, students, support people, individuals with professional counseling skills, administrators, copastors, and codirectors. We were all Welcome Inn friends who contributed and at the same time received.

Was this emphasis already part of the "new card game" that Renee suggested? I did have to admit that the client imagery was often still present in our ministry.

I remember a games evening at the center that illustrated the possibility of a new card game. The main room was filled to capacity, with a good mix of educated and well-to-do volunteers and people who struggled daily with personal poverty issues. I noticed in particular the laughter at a table of four who were playing cards.

There sat Jim and Kathleen, a couple living in subsidized housing in the Survey. Jim, who was in his late forties, had never completed high school. After twenty years of hard work building train cars for a steel company, he had been laid off. For at least five years, the most he had been able to find was occasional work as a laborer. Kathleen suffered from depression and was under constant treatment. Jim did all the cooking and most of the parenting for their five teenagers, who demanded much attention.

Across from them at the card table sat Henri and Sue. Henri was a successful personnel administrator who was always advancing to more demanding positions that took him into situations with high-ranking civic officials. Sue, also well-educated, was a professional music teacher; attending concerts was important to her. The cost of one of their evenings out would have easily eaten up several weeks of Jim and Kathleen's grocery money. The economic divide was colossal, as dramatic as in the story Jesus told of the rich man and Lazarus (Luke 16:19-31). I often wrestled with such inequities and wondered how they could be rectified.

This time, however, I was overwhelmed by the laughter as the group of four shuffled their cards. I no longer saw them as volunteers and people on public assistance—as merely a wealthy couple giving their time to the happy recipients of a generous gift.

I discovered a miracle taking place right in our midst. All four were enjoying themselves immensely, joking with each other, their masks dropped. True friendship was being fostered. Indeed, a new card game was being played. Was this the card game Jesus was talking about when he said, "I have called you friends" (John 15:15)?

The Two-Dollar Card

Frank was a troubled single man with many psychological problems. Occasionally, he arrived at church wearing women's clothing and carrying a large, purple purse. He never seemed to have any money but lived in various places: on the streets, in his own rented room, in a shelter, or with his sister, who was also on disability.

Sometimes when he came to worship at the center, I mumbled a quick prayer: "God, please don't let him disrupt the service again."

On one occasion, he came in late, immediately marched to the front, and offered to sing a song. Before I could respond, he began singing "Amazing Grace." The sanctuary suddenly became silent as his voice filled the room. All the unholy chatter, along with the order of worship for the day, disintegrated as we were left to breathe in the Spirit in pure form. The presence and miraculous power of the Holy One left no one untouched. Frank's clear tenor voice matched that of any professional singer. That morning, he became our Ben Heppner (the Canadian tenor who performs in the world's foremost opera and concert halls).

One evening Doreen and I were relaxing, playing a game of Scrabble. My kids had reminded me that it was the day before my birthday. We heard a quick knock on the door, and there was Frank, all excited.

"I've got something for you!"

Soon he was seated at our kitchen table and the coffeepot was on. Frank could hardly wait to hand me the envelope. His eyes beamed with satisfaction, and his white teeth glowed in a broad grin that contrasted with his dark complexion. "This is all I have," he cried out.

The card read:

A special birthday greeting
that someone gladly sends,
not just because your birthday's here,
but more because we're friends.

In his handwriting were the scribbled words, "To Hugo, God bless always, from Frank." Tumbling out of the envelope came two one-dollar bills, along with some loose change.

I must confess my first reaction was similar to Judas's in John 12:1-8: Frank, the card's okay, but the precious cash . . . you shouldn't have. You don't have a lot of money. You're poor, and you don't know how to budget. Where will you get money for breakfast tomorrow? Frank, it's foolish to give what you yourself need. *Why wasn't this money given to the poor?*

I was clearly mimicking Judas, who criticized Mary for offering her gift of expensive perfume. "But no," I thought. "I don't want to be like Judas. I'm not that kind of guy. Or am I?"

Also in that story was Mary, whom Jesus affirmed in front of all the criticizers. What lavish and surpassing love to present Jesus with that special, costly fragrance!

And Frank, what gracious love you have shown me. You have given everything you have!

Suddenly, a powerful, new warmth filled the room. The scene of Mary's generous gift to her Savior was replayed right in our own home.

Doreen and I invited Frank to the piano. We sang and laughed and fellowshipped into the night, forgetting about the time. After a rather exuberant song, Frank burst out, "I haven't had this much fun in a long time!"

We chimed in, "Neither have we!"

All of a sudden, Frank looked at his watch. Then he looked outside. It was totally dark. I sensed him thinking about the long walk home and about how he should have left earlier. But it was so good to be there with him.

He fumbled in his pockets, took out his wallet, opened it, and shook it. It was empty. After a moment of hesitation he gently asked, "Would you be able to spare me some money for bus fare?"

We gladly gave him the money, two dollars—a different two dollars—and with "God bless you," he was on his way. A new kind of giving and receiving, reinforced by the Mary and Jesus story, had been etched in the deepest parts of our souls.

I still have the two dollars he gave me, stapled to the inside of the birthday card.

A Forced Offer of Purchase

The letter from City Hall addressed to the codirectors looked kind of official, so I put down the fluorescent light bulb I was changing and tore open the envelope. We had applied for a government grant to fund a student project, and I thought this might be the answer. My heart beat rapidly in anticipation.

I pored quickly through the contents and hardly believed my eyes when I saw the word *expropriation*. The city was threatening to take away our building. The center that had shown hospitality to so many people was to be vacated by the first of January, only a few months away. The old brick building with its classic storefront display windows and recessed doorway, once known as Dorothy's Dry Goods, was falling victim to urban renewal.

For almost six years, the Welcome Inn sign had swayed in the wind as it hung invitingly from the edge of the roof and beckoned all to a place where friends would meet friends and strangers would become friends. We had thought that purchasing the building four years earlier would ensure the center's presence in the community more permanently. The center's funds were very limited, but we had recently put in several thousand dollars worth of electrical wiring and hoped that a major renovation project would radically transform the old building while keeping its historical luster.

The urban renewal program was rapidly tearing down many of the city's oldest buildings, and remaining housing was at a premium. Many of the buildings that could have served as meeting space were already demolished or had been grabbed up by businesses. I doubted we could find sufficient space for the compensation the city was offering. The letter also said that if we did not immediately accept the offer, the city would proceed toward expropriation.

I suddenly knew firsthand what some of my North End friends had experienced. At first, I hadn't fully believed the stories when I talked with a family who had received such a notice. But it soon became apparent that, after months of badgering by City Hall, such families moved out of the area and we rarely saw them again. Most had not been able to find accommodations as good as those they were leaving. Was this what "urban renewal" was supposed to mean?

Like our friends from the neighborhood, we too were powerless. Or were we? When I took the letter to our board meeting, I soon discovered the many resources available to us. Within a few days, we had a well-known lawyer working for us and had negotiated a much higher price, in addition to a deadline extension. People willing to help us find a new location emerged. After much searching, we moved into a large house with a suitable walkout basement, located only blocks from the original building.

Some time later Roxanna, a single mom with six children, called me. "I've just got to buy my own place. I'm sick and tired of fixing up place after place, and just when I'm comfortable, the landlord decides to sell. Can you help me?"

I remembered all the help the center had received when our building was expropriated. And my own parents had helped our family with a loan when we purchased our North End home. Were we not all of the same stock? Our center had brought all kinds of people together from a variety of backgrounds and economic means. Should there not be more equality among us? I resolved to put my energy into helping this single mom on public assistance buy a permanent home.

It wasn't easy. But I was on a mission, and nothing would deter me. My research showed that government grants were available for first-time homebuyers. But the program was designed for people with jobs. Still I forged ahead. I put Roxanna in touch with housing officials and gave her suggestions on real-estate matters. In short, I became an advocate for her. I faced skeptics with many prejudices against people on welfare. Numerous roadblocks almost caused me to give up. Finally, my determination paid off, and with the help of an understanding real-estate agent and government personnel, Roxanna purchased her first house.

The *good news to the poor* that our center stood for had gone beyond the announcement stage. But did it have to take the threat of losing our own building to help me take on a new form of reign-of-God construction? Maybe, just maybe, God was smiling and saying, "I'm not finished with you yet. There are more new card games to learn."

A Conversation with an Old-Timer

I had met an older gentleman named Harry when I had gone into Bay Auto Wreckers to find a used windshield-wiper motor for our old car, which always seemed to be in need of repair. He usually sat on an old van seat that his business very aptly had supplied for him. When I rode my bike on my visits in the neighborhood, I would sometimes stop and say hello to this old-timer.

"Tell me, Harry," I once asked him, "what was it like to grow up in the North End?"

Harry told me how they used to swim in the large bay at the westerly point of Lake Ontario. "Every weekend people from all over the city would join us for one grand party. The water was clean. We swam, we fished, and in winter we played hockey. It was like our playground."

"What's happened?" I asked.

"Well, just take a look. Where can you get to the water-front? From the skyway you've got about ten miles of steel companies. They spill their garbage into the air and into the water. Then there's a number of private yacht clubs that nobody around here can afford. Looking west you've got two miles of train tracks that circle up past the high-level bridge. And then, for Pete's sake, we have the cemetery on the other side. So where do I get to the water?"

I mentally followed the geography. "I guess you're right," I said. "You've been shut out. But the water is so dirty now.

You wouldn't really want to go swimming in it anyway."

"I hear that they are wanting to clean up the water. Those politicians are even boasting that in five years we'll be able to drink from the bay. That's rubbish. Once you kill everything with that slag, it's gone forever."

"What about the park they just put in?"

"Oh yes, that's open to us. A tiny sliver of a park, squished between the clubs. And I guess you can get to the water right behind Bay Street. That's where the Lax brothers have filled in the bay to create about ten acres of land. I don't pay attention to the no-trespassing sign. I go back there for memory's sake. I hear there's a group of business people who want to build a small city of high-rises on the landfill. That will double the population of the North End."

"But can the North End sustain so many more people?" I asked. "What about traffic and schools and the infrastructure that would be required?"

"Yeah, I agree, but city hall doesn't pay a lot of attention to us. You say you're on a committee of North Enders who are working toward a healthier neighborhood. Good luck to you. You've got your work cut out for you."

Doreen and I saw more and more that our Christian presence in the North End would require a commitment to helping our neighbors participate in decisions that affected them. As some of us from the center worked on various neighborhood committees, we were pleased that more access to the waterfront and a cleaner bay were gradually being placed on politicians' agenda. By identifying with those living below the poverty line, listening to their stories of loss and powerlessness, and becoming active in their concerns, our credibility as conveyors of the story of Jesus of Nazareth was also growing stronger.

A Twist to the Good Samaritan Story

We had come together from various service ministries in southern Ontario to listen to one another and to examine the familiar story of the good Samaritan (Luke 10:25-37). In the room were about forty friends, all of whom were living on some form of public assistance.

There was Linda, a single mom with two children, who had come out of a very abusive relationship a number of years ago. She was a remarkable community leader. Living in the same low-income housing project was Janine, also single, who worked for minimum wage at McDonald's. Reg had a university degree in physics, but had been unable to find employment. He had an obsession with buying books; once his landlord had threatened to evict him from his second-floor apartment because the floor was beginning to sag from the stacks of books. Coming from a well-to-do family but then abandoned by them, at eighteen Arlene had been hit by a car that had left her battered body with symptoms resembling cerebral palsy. Lucinda, a newcomer to Canada from Guatemala, was studying English as a second language. Many had experienced much hurt in their lives. The heartfelt words of one of our North End friends still often grabs my attention: "The suffering, the stress, is terrible when you can't work and have to depend on welfare."

Also there were several dozen individuals involved as staff or volunteers in service ministries. These were people with a strong Christian motivation to help, but who also struggled with various issues in their lives. What an extraordinary blend of people to be in the same room—not what I had been accustomed to growing up!

After a dramatic presentation of the good Samaritan story, we divided into small groups with the assignment to list and examine the various personalities in the narrative. The final question was, "With whom do you most identify in this story?"

The responses were most interesting. Almost all of the well-to-do volunteers and staff identified with one of three characters. Some immediately chose the priest or the Levite, who had abandoned the victim and circled by on the other side. They felt guilty about not doing enough for people in need, though they affirmed an impulse to bandage wounds and offer assistance. A few dared to see themselves in the questioning mode of the lawyer.

In contrast, a majority of those with few financial resources chose to identify with the traveler who had fallen among the thieves, someone with whom I had never thought of identifying.

"How so?" I couldn't keep myself from asking.

"My kids were robbed of having piano lessons," said Linda. "There was no money for that. Or for going on some of the school trips. Most of the time I kept my kids home, saying they were sick. I just didn't have the extra cash."

"It's the same for me," Lucinda responded, "I'm a refugee, and people stole my neat little house in the country. Coming to Canada, I'm still finding it difficult to locate affordable housing. I thought education would get me a job, but I haven't got one yet."

Person after person spoke of being in the victim category. But for them the hope in the story was obvious. Jesus never wanted people to remain victims. Though their reality had sometimes been to see religious establishments and church people pass on the other side, they saw that this was not God's intention.

The good Samaritan tale took on new meaning that day for a group of middle-class people because they had examined Scripture alongside those who were poor. I contemplated what other new biblical insights might be there for us.

Voices to the Decision Makers

Imagine you feel trapped in a social system designed by others to help you. Although you recognize the benefits of welfare, daily you feel its inadequacies, which you have little power to do anything about. For a seminary course I once interviewed ten of my Welcome Inn friends and asked them what it was like to be on public assistance. Their comments reflected what I often heard while living in the North End.

> It makes me feel like I'm mooching off the government. I want to be on my own. I want to earn something.

> I live in fear because of the guilt trip society places on me for raising my children on welfare.

> It's like not having enough for things I need, and that makes me angry.

> It's being broke all the time.

> It hurts so much to be classified in a certain category. It's too much for me. Why? I was taught at home not to categorize.

> Being poor is demeaning. It's always rubbed in. I feel like a tree within a world, all alone.

I live in fear, fear of not having enough money at the end
of the month. It shouldn't be that way in this country.

When our center was asked to present the thoughts of
those who were living below the poverty line to a government-
sponsored commission reviewing social-assistance programs,
we called together persons living on public assistance, and this
was our presentation:

Recommendations to the Provincial Social Assistance Review Committee by the Friends of Welcome Inn Living Below the Poverty Line

We are a group of people living below the poverty line
and representing the working poor, the disabled, those
on family benefits, those on welfare, the unemployed
and the underemployed, those in lodging homes, and
those between sixty and sixty-five years who experience a special hardship. Thank you for this opportunity to present to you some of our concerns and recommendations on the welfare system in Ontario.

We appreciate some aspects of the programs designed
to help us, such as medical care under OHIP (Ontario
Health Insurance Plan) available to everyone in
Ontario. The fact that we do have an income, as inadequate as it may be, is helpful. As one member in our
group put it, "Some income is better than no income."
However, we still find many hardships connected with
being on assistance. Many of us have a lot of fear and
anger that we haven't even begun to express.
"Welfare," as one of us recently stated, "makes us feel
low and little," when it should rather be encouraging
us in our self-worth.

The following are some of our recommendations:

1. We would like to be seen as full participants in our society and would like to see policies that support the low-income group in that direction. All people are created in God's image, which means having dignity and self-worth. This is not possible when we are treated as recipients and are called that. We also are contributors and want to be recognized as such. We wish for opportunities to give as well as receive.

   a. There needs to be massive restructuring of government priorities so that meaningful, good quality, reasonable-paying jobs become available to everyone. We are unhappy with government officials who state we will need to learn to live with 8 percent unemployment. Full employment, full participation needs to be the goal of our wealthy society.

   b. There need to be more options for training, retraining, and upgrading that will lead to meaningful, adequately paid employment. This also includes individuals who may only be able to work part-time.

   c. There needs to be recognition of the value of homemaking, and if a mother or father chooses to be at home with the family, our social-service system needs to support these efforts with money, resources, and moral support.

   d. There needs to be much more economic and social encouragement given to those who are moving from assistance to full-time or part-time employment. So often, those who wish to improve their economic situations are penalized by having money deducted from their Social Assistance checks.

e. Individuals working in sheltered workshops should receive a decent wage so they can be more independent.

2. We would like to see that information on Social Assistance be written in language that we can understand and that this information be readily available to all.

3. The right to appeal procedures needs to be clearly described to those who receive Social Assistance. It should also be available in writing in an easy-to-read pamphlet form.

4. We would like to be able to express our views on policies that affect us. Many of us have given up speaking for change because we have not felt we were listened to. Can the Social Allowance policies not encourage the policy makers to listen to those of us on low-income and include us in the setting of policies?

5. The lack of suitable, affordable housing is a crisis for those of us on low income. We encourage the government to give higher priority to increasing the amount of available housing for rent and for purchase. Low-income people have few options, and often are left spending 50 percent of their checks on rent or living in very undesirable housing.

6. We believe that in our country of wealth, everyone should be able to have an adequate financial income structured to the total needs of the family. Social allowances need to be raised immediately to the National Council on Welfare poverty line so that every Canadian is assured of a decent standard of living. Presently we experience hardships in the following areas:

a. Housing—Many of us pay much more rent and utilities than is allowed for that purpose in our checks.

b. Food—Many of us find ourselves out of food during the last two weeks of the month and need to beg for grocery handouts. This becomes very difficult for us to do, but it is our only way to survive.

c. Transportation—We often walk because we cannot afford to purchase bus passes or buy a vehicle.

d. Extra Fees—Many of us do not have funds to pay for our children's school trips, hockey practices, music lessons, or for our entertainment, appliance repairs, etc.

As one member in our group put it, "The government needs to get away from saying, 'Let's add a little here and a little there,' but let the government just ensure that we receive an adequate fair income, as other Canadians do."

Thank you for listening to us.[13]

Could it be that the voices of the poor and marginalized in our country and our world are just waiting to be heard? I visualize thousands of small groups and forums taking place across our country, where the well-to-do sit with the poor, not to prescribe solutions, but to hear their stories. Would our places of worship, our use of financial resources, our educational facilities, and yes the fabric of our society, be any different if we took seriously the council of those who are poor?

A Journey on the Bruce Trail

Being fully immersed in the life of the North End was challenging and exciting. New situations always needed attention:

•A family of four was in crisis because they couldn't find a decent place to live. They were temporarily staying with friends in a house designed for one small family.

•A teenager from the Survey had broken into the corner store and stolen cigarettes and candy. Now a probation officer was calling for someone to spend time with the teen.

•A work bee had to be organized to help one of the families whose housekeeping standards had fallen apart beyond belief, and the Child Protection agency was strongly suggesting that they may need to take the children into care.

•People who came to the center wanted us to have more intergenerational family events, so planning was needed.

•Because of the innovative activities at the center, the university called us requesting additional field placements for their social-work students.

More and more programs were emerging at the center. We constantly worked at acquiring an expanded volunteer pool and long-term staff. The local neighborhood organization asked me to be on its board. I was deeply involved in the peace movement, organizing and participating in peace and poverty walks, together with friends from the center. Our home was also open to the community, with people phoning us and dropping in for coffee and kids from the street asking for help with their go-carts. The center's community of faith was another powerful, growing movement. New people were added to the congregation almost every week.

Living and working in the neighborhood, being on call twenty-four hours a day, seven days a week, and being needed by the North End was a wonderful affirmation for me. People appreciated the leadership team Doreen and I were. Our skills and gifts were called on from all circles: local people, educators, landlords, staff, supporting churches and conferences, and even politicians. More and more we were being accepted as North Enders and it was good to hear people say, "Hugo and Doreen are part of us." But for me, all was not well.

A tearful plea by my eight-year-old son, Tim, as I was about to leave the house stopped me in my tracks. "You're going out again? I want you to fix my train track."

Earlier over supper, I had argued with Doreen and had not felt good about my angry outbursts, especially in front of the kids. Doreen and I always had a very good relationship and continued to grow in our love for one another as we worked through conflicts. We felt called to serve in a united way and were strongly committed to each other and to a God of love. But lately our communication patterns had slid to about a 25-percent level. What was happening to me? Did I need a Sabbath? A book called *Sabbath Time: Understanding and Practice for Contemporary Christians* that a long-time friend had given me lay untouched on the shelf.

As I walked home from a meeting that night, I reflected on a board member's comment that I had not been "with it" and that they had "almost lost me." I realized I was beginning to burn out. From the encounter with my family earlier in the evening it was obvious that they were feeling the brunt of it. But I didn't take the signs seriously and was soon caught up again in the busy life of community ministry.

Some time later, after another busy weekend of community activities, I woke up early one Monday morning. I considered whether to take the day off or go in to work to complete the numerous tasks that were waiting, including the inevitable emergencies that would come up. Almost in a stupor, I told Doreen I was going to take some Sabbath time. I decided to walk the spectacular Bruce Trail, which wound along the beautiful Niagara escarpment and made a giant horseshoe around Hamilton.

"I feel compelled to go," I told her, and she agreed to pick me up at a designated spot later that evening.

I began the day by walking directly south from our house, across the tracks, through downtown. I made my way up the 120-meter escarpment that splits the city, and was on the trail within ninety minutes. All day I walked and meditated as I passed trees of brilliant orange, red, and green, and every autumn shade in between. Small streams and the occasional cascading waterfall graced the carpeted forest floor. I often peeked through the trees on the crest and viewed the city below. I sometimes even captured a glimpse of what I thought was the tallest church in the North End.

I walked all day. But more significantly, I talked to my Creator, the God of the city, who spoke to me. Then I knew what I had to do.

First thing on Tuesday I phoned my Catholic friend, Sister Helen, who was part of the peace movement. I told her that I thought we should begin a prayer group. She said that she had been praying the night before and had received the exact same inspiration. Another friend, Margaret, a Quaker, was also not surprised by the suggestion. She had been about to telephone me when she received my call. A third friend, Paul, a Baptist professor, was also moved in that direction. Within an hour, six people had agreed to meet once a week at seven in the morning for an hour of prayer. Social issues would not be discussed, no planning would take place; we would devote ourselves fully to silent meditation and prayer.

This prayer group would go on to meet for about five years. Doreen also joined us. Most interesting about those years was the appreciation I gained for healthy Sabbath rest in my life. My quiet time with other people active in social ministry gave a new perspective on all that I was doing. I began to learn not only to *do*, but also to *be*. My family suddenly saw in me a more contented disposition and a new respect for their needs. My relationship with Doreen deepened. Soon we regularly took a day off for reflection, renewal, and recreation.

Early during the weekly one-hour periods of silence, God spoke to me in powerful ways. I became motivated, with God's help, to avoid burnout. Today I thank God for the miraculous way in which a day on the trail, followed by a prayer group, helped me to rediscover the Sabbath.

–5–
Wasn't It Like a Fire Burning?

When he was at the table with them, [Jesus] took bread, blessed and broke it, and gave it to them. Then their eyes were opened, and they recognized him; and he vanished from their sight. They said to each other, "Were not our hearts burning within us while he was talking to us on the road, while he was opening the scriptures to us?"

That same hour they got up and returned to Jerusalem; and they found the eleven and their companions gathered together. They were saying, "The Lord has risen indeed, and he has appeared to Simon!" Then they told what had happened on the road, and how he had been made known to them in the breaking of the bread.

While they were talking about this, Jesus himself stood among them and said to them, "Peace be with you." *(Luke 24:30-36)*

This is where we are most unjust to our poor—we don't know them. We don't know how great they are, how lovable, how hungry for that understanding love. . . . Today God is loving the world through you and through me and through all those who are his love and compassion in the world.[14]

—*Mother Teresa*

From a Rock Garden to a Garden Built on a Rock

Once upon a time there was a small, urban Mennonite congregation in southern Ontario. Like many church plants, the community was birthed by a number of like-minded people from similar backgrounds who had moved to the city for employment and career options. Many drove a fair distance to worship in this particular congregation, with its Anabaptist values of careful biblical discernment, the caring community of faith, and practical discipleship based on the way of peace taught and lived by Jesus.[15] Teachers, cabinetmakers, social workers, health-care professionals, company executives, secretaries, researchers, and others became the pioneers who formed Hamilton Mennonite Church.

Weekly attendance was soon at about forty people. With the help of the wider Mennonite denomination, the members began to construct a church building in the university area of the city. Designed by a budding Mennonite architect, it included many modern features, such as a circular worship space that helped to create a community atmosphere. Instead of pews, it had moveable chairs. The building itself was to blend in with the neighborhood and was to be focused on people, not on the steeple.

Since Hamilton was known for its Royal Botanical Gardens, originally begun through the transformation of an old quarry, the congregation decided to feature an attractive rock garden along the back and side of the church. This could be done easily, since the church lot had a gentle slope to it. It was said that this unique rock garden would fit in with the local Hamilton scene and would help to attract new people to the church.

The new building and its innovative characteristics brought the church members together, and the congregation slowly began to grow. At first the increase came as people of Mennonite background joined, but others soon identified with the church because of its emphasis on a caring, creative faith community that took seriously the call to peace and justice.

During the construction phase, many people put in many hours of volunteer time. They began to ask some tough questions: Why are we here? What is our purpose? Are we too focused on ourselves? Their pastor challenged them in a sermon to explore a local ministry in which all could participate.

While completing the final touches on their beautiful building, they met to pray, discuss, and discern where they could concretely reach out to people beyond their congregation. In their search they interviewed city officials, the police, probation officers, social service people, business people, professors in the nearby expanding university, and whoever might be able to identify needs.

Eventually, they were directed to one of the oldest sections of the city, eight kilometers from the church's middle-class neighborhood, where a major urban renewal project was underway. They talked to local residents and storeowners as they walked the streets of the old inner city. The congregation eventually decided to begin the adventure by opening a center in Hamilton's North End. An old storefront along busy James Street North that still bore the name Dorothy's Dry Goods would serve nicely as a meeting place, they decided.

The center was called Welcome Inn, a named that suggested hospitality, like the inns of old. The goal was simply stated:

"To be a Christian presence in an area of need." A VS unit was established, where youth and older people could volunteer. The workers were invited to see their role as helping the congregation in its new ministry.

Soon the old storefront was bustling with all kinds of activity. People dropped in for emergency help, women's sewing classes, children's clubs, or simply came to chat over a cup of coffee. Congregation members found themselves interacting with dozens and dozens of unchurched people, many of whom were ravaged by poverty and found new hope through the presence of church members and VSers volunteering hours and hours of their time. Something quite pronounced was beginning to happen.

But the rock garden was not receiving the attention for which it had been designed, because members of the congregation had been drawn to ministry in another part of the city. One day, a work bee was organized to spruce up the neglected garden. A work event had been planned on the same day to repair homes for needy persons in the North End. There was potential for a major conflict and some hard feelings.

God's sense of humor about what to do with the rock garden soon became apparent. The garden was falling into disrepair; it was not being watered and had gradually attracted more and more weeds. It was not drawing new people to the congregation but was becoming an eyesore.

One day someone pointed out a hole in the parking lot of the church. The hole seemed to be getting bigger and bigger, sucking in the gravel. We soon discovered that the cover of an old buried well a few feet below the surface had rotted out. It occurred to a number of us that we could get rid of the dangerous situation and take care of the garden at the same time.

"Why don't we just throw the rock garden down the drain?" someone suggested.

So the church people carried the rocks one by one from the

garden and dropped them into the hole until all were gone and the old well was filled.

With a strong sense of local ministry and an ongoing involvement in the Welcome Inn Center, the congregation of Hamilton Mennonite Church grew. To accommodate the growing membership, an addition to the building was erected on the site of the old garden. A congregation with a rock garden began a new garden, the Welcome Inn, built on the solid Rock.

The Welcome Inn Is My Church

The mandate for Doreen and I as codirectors of the Welcome Inn was to be a Christian presence. This was written into our job description and we clearly embraced it. Our mentor, Herman Enns, pastor of Hamilton Mennonite Church, once said: "The evangelism of the Bible is beautiful. It first of all responds to the basic needs of persons, who then begin to experience not only the love from another human being, but also the supreme God of love."

I liked this approach. Responding to immediate needs meant many things. It meant using our rusting car to deliver a donated mattress, or move an entire family forced to vacate their home, or give someone a ride to the social services office downtown, or taking someone to a doctor. (When we first arrived in the North End, there was not a single doctor's office in the area.) It also meant providing groceries or grocery money to supplement inadequate government assistance.

Often it meant walking with people as they confronted an oppressive welfare system. I remember coming home from a Social Assistance appeal hearing and saying to Doreen, "Well, it took all day, but we were able to save Mrs. Kitchen eight hundred dollars." That was a lot of money for a mother with six children who depended on every penny of her welfare check. The agency had claimed to have made an overpayment to her and was taking fifty dollars off her allowance every month to make up for it. Mrs. Kitchen had argued profusely with a social services worker, insisting that the department had made a mistake. She eventually came to me. "Help me go to the top. I know I must appeal their decision," she pleaded.

The sincerity in her request was obvious to me, and I knew I must use my resources to help. I listened carefully to Mrs. Kitchen and asked her to spell out in writing the situation from her perspective. With this documentation and the formal appeal I helped her work out, the officers clearly could not brush her aside. It turned out that the department had made a mistake and that there had not been an overpayment. They apologized for not listening to Mrs. Kitchen's pleas.

One day I decided to do a follow-up visit to Marianne and her seven children. A few weeks before I had found the whole family on a very chilly day huddled together on a large bed in the living room because there was no heat in the house. We eventually managed to get the gas turned back on after paying the past-due bill.

Marianne greeted me in all seriousness. "Well, here comes my Mennonite priest. Thanks so much for helping us with the heat."

I was a VSer at the time and saw my role as simply giving a hand to those in need, so it was shocking to have her identify me with an official title of the church.

I corrected her. "No, I'm certainly not a priest. Besides, we don't call our spiritual leaders priests. We just say pastors, and I'm not a pastor."

"But you are with the church, aren't you?"

"Well, yes, but I'm really a social worker. We're just trying to be helpful wherever we are called."

"I gave up on the church awhile ago, but I know you must believe in God. Why would you have helped me when you saw our house was so cold?"

I said nothing, and we went on to other topics. I was too

timid to clearly acknowledge my honest and deep Christian motivation for service.

Later I puzzled over those words "Mennonite priest." Did they mean anything? Could the things I was doing be identified as pastoral? Surely it didn't mean that I was to become a pastor? Though in my Bible college and university years I had felt some affinity toward pastoral ministry, I had become preoccupied with the social-work direction.

About a year later, a number of us were walking home from the center after an evening program of crafts for adults. At that time the emphasis at the center was on service, with only the occasional devotional when it seemed appropriate. It was always fun to join the folks walking home, since it afforded a time of communal reflection.

As we talked about the good time we'd had, Teresa, who had been benefiting from the ministry almost from its beginning said, "You know, the Welcome Inn is my church." Others in the group agreed. I smiled silently inside as I remembered how a few of these people had told me they had been hurt by the church and would never again set foot inside a church door.

But questions still lingered for me. There's no church building, there's no Sunday school, no Bible study, no pastor or priest, not even a worship service. How can it be your church?

Teresa continued, "I bring my whole family to the children's groups, and we go to the family outings. I love the Monday-night women's quilting group, and my husband comes to the men's club. We're like a family here. We help each other out and share what we have, and we believe God loves us."

Not long after that I was asked to lead in a memorial service for the stillborn child of a young, unmarried girl named Amy, a restless teenager whose superficial relationship with a young man had long since dissolved. She and her family were left to bear their grief alone. They had no church, but felt the "church" aspect in the programs at the center.

It was difficult to know what to say on such an occasion. I decided that in the service, which was to be at a funeral home, I would be as genuine as possible, emphasizing God's generosity within our brokenness. The warmth I received from the family touched me deeply.

As more pastoral requests came to me and Doreen, a group at the center suggested that we get together to "talk more church." We hesitantly posted a notice on the bulletin board among all the other announcements that said we would begin a series of evening meetings with those interested in talking about "the deeper questions of life." Many people who came to the center discouraged us from being too religious, so we wanted to make sure this movement was coming from within and was authentically of God. We prayed and studied our Bibles at home, but came to our sessions with an open mind to hear about the people's struggles.

Attempts had been made to refer people to churches in the neighborhood. Our relationship with those congregations was positive, and together we had even developed some major summer programming. However, the push at the center was for a more unconventional worship style than what those congregations provided. And it was unrealistic to expect many of our Welcome Inn friends to attend churches where they didn't know anyone.

The Welcome Inn Church started with a small nucleus of folks who could candidly talk about their questions, but it soon blossomed into a dynamic, imaginative worshipping community. In a natural and unhurried way, Doreen and I also grew in our pastoral skills.

After a year of discernment in the local and wider community, we were ordained as pastors in the Mennonite Church. It was a beautiful ceremony, with many Welcome Inn friends taking an active part. Most touching was spontaneous sharing by Gregory, who read in his broken English, "How beautiful are the feet of those who bring the good news" (Romans 10:15). The pastoral calling into which we had reluctantly stepped was being affirmed. We felt the fire burning inside.

My Interrupted Peace Sermon

A preaching course I took at McMaster Divinity College demanded that I not only think through the content of my message but also examine the way I presented it. While some of the readings and lectures didn't seem to apply to the informal worship setting at the center, I found it helpful to learn to purposefully integrate biblical material with what was going on right in our neighborhood.

One day I was working at a small desk in a bedroom overlooking our narrow lot on Simcoe Street. I struggled with a sermon on Ephesians 6:15, in which Paul compels us to put on shoes that will make us "ready to proclaim the gospel of peace." What excellent imagery Paul had come up with, I thought. I envisioned myself dancing through the streets of the North End, leaving footprints of peace everywhere I went. On the other hand, I could also picture myself in heavily plated army boots, taking on aggression and authoritarian practices that could cause havoc in relationships.

I heard a commotion outside—a scuffle, and angry voices. I trembled as I looked out my upstairs window and froze in a bent position at the ledge. Right next to our front steps, but on the neighbor's property, two grown men were smashing another man's face onto the rough cement of the driveway, holding his hands behind his back. A third person was brandishing a thick iron rod over his head, ready to strike him at any moment.

The chasm between the violent scene outside and the theological thoughts I'd been contemplating was just too great. I was totally immobilized, stooped there in fear. It was as if all my emotions and intellect had been squished into a bowl and sealed with a tight lid. I couldn't get to the phone and call 911. I couldn't pray. Visions of a brutal murder appeared before me, and I shook. Finally, I sank to the floor and closed my eyes.

Violence always does something to me, like it does to everyone. It unleashes anger and retaliation. It intensifies injustice and often takes on a volatility of its own. It causes enormous physical trauma and unspeakable social and psychological damage, producing alienation, broken relationships, and war. Violence does all this and more, because it flies in the face of a loving and just God who says, "But I say to you, Love your enemies and pray for those who persecute you, so that you may be children of your Father who is in heaven" (Matthew 5:44-45a).

In my state of shock I couldn't bring any of Jesus's words of peace to my consciousness. Not even close at hand were the familiar words of Paul in 1 Corinthians 13: "Love is patient; love is kind: love is not envious or boastful or arrogant or rude." My "shoes of peace" sermon seemed disconnected from my life experience. Or was it?

As I cautiously looked out the window again, the aggressors backed off and allowed the pinned man to slowly get to his feet and trudge down the street. I stared motionless. Then relief took over my body and soul. A multitude of questions lingered amid that welcoming solace.

A few days later, after getting home late from a meeting, we were again reminded of the challenges right next door. We turned on the television and noticed the camera focused on our neighbor's house, with our own house in the background. The reporter announced that the police had shot our neighbor's two pit bulls and had arrested Louie on drug charges. Doreen and I glanced at each other, finally realizing why so many cars drove in and out of his driveway, stopping a few moments for transactions.

I had first met Louie when he began renting the large cement-block garage at the back of the lot next door for his unofficial auto-body repair business. I began talking to him over the fence. He noticed our deteriorating, rusted vehicle and offered to replace the front driver's door, which showed the most damage. He did a good job, and we were blessed that we had to pay him only a fraction of the going rate. A few times he invited me into the front of the garage, where we sat on old couches as we chatted. One day I saw him with a huge bruise on the side of his face and an ugly black eye. But he explained it as a work-related accident, though I wondered if that was true.

I don't know what his connection was, if any, to the fellows I had seen fighting from my upstairs window. The crime underworld spins a complicated web. But how does one relate to people caught up in drug trafficking? Surely the good news is also for them.

Louie disappeared after his arrest. I never saw the other fellows again either. Was there some follow-up "Christian presence" ministry I could still do?

I learned profoundly that peace thoughts and peace actions need to be closely intertwined. In spite of a theology that emphasizes loving an enemy, when it comes right down to it, we can never be in control of the outcome in violent situations. Neither do we know how we will respond. But when we have invited Jesus, the Prince of Peace, to walk alongside us and we work daily at fostering a peaceful existence, there is a difference. We will more readily respond in helpful ways, even when there doesn't seem to be a resolution.

Lord, I Just Had a Fight with My Wife

We had hurried to get ourselves and our four boys bundled up for church.

"Gerald and Tim, did you remember to bring the canned goods for the food bank collection during the offering time?"

"Sheldon, don't forget to brush your teeth, and Jonathan, this is the last time I'm telling you to get your shoes and jacket on."

"Doreen, we need to hurry up. I hate to be late for church." Sometimes the pressure of getting ready so frazzled me that all my peace theology took a severe beating.

On this day I was the speaker, while others from the neighborhood led worship and took part in other aspects of the service. From the beginning of the faith community, it had seemed natural to include members in the leadership of the services.

North End friends were not shy in expressing their views. Once my cousin John gave a dynamic sermon and kept everyone on the edge of their chairs. One of the first comments I received after the service was, "You should preach like that." By then I wasn't as intimidated as in the past and was learning to take criticism with grace.

Dennis was leading worship for the first time. He was a family man who always brought his three children, his wife, and sometimes neighbors or relatives to church with him. His asthma had forced him to leave his job with a manufacturing company, and he had only occasional work. He often lamented his inability to provide financially for his family, but I assured him that he was still a good father and husband, and he seemed encouraged.

A small band consisting of guitar, flute, harmonica, tambourines, and a homemade, one-string washtub bass played by Raymond, a fellow on disability, began to quiet the seventy-five folks assembled for worship. The warm greetings, hugs, and animated conversations turned the setting into a joyful, family-reunion-style atmosphere. Newcomers always seemed to be present, as well as some who hadn't been around for a while. All were welcomed.

Just a few moments after the designated starting time, Dennis confidently strode to the podium. All eyes turned to him. Feeling somewhat responsible, I tended to be a little anxious about how new leaders would carry out their tasks.

He began, "Would everyone please pray with me?" He paused for a long time, and I momentarily thought I might have to step in. But then with charisma and a strong, clear voice cracking with deep sincerity, he prayed: "Lord, I just had a fight with my wife. It's been crazy! What a terrible week I've had. But I'm here, just as I am. I know I get myself into all these messes, but you know all of us do this sometimes."

There was a long pause.

"But, Lord, we're here to worship you, to give you honor and praise. Be with all of us today. We want to listen to you. Amen."

My immediate inner reaction was, Why did we ask Dennis to lead worship? This guy is unstable. We don't need someone to reinforce the personal problems in our faith community, where most people have gone through so much trauma. We need someone strong to lead.

What I was really thinking was that we needed someone strong like me. I grew up in a church where spiritual leaders were generally seen as exemplary people with many gifts. All my training and experience reinforced such a position. Personal problems needed to be dealt with elsewhere.

I noticed that no one else seemed bothered by this call to worship. As the Holy Spirit typically works in settings of worship, my defensiveness gradually softened in my second reaction. Pure honesty with God began to take hold of me. I suddenly recalled my argumentative tone earlier in the morning. Yes, more then once I had had a fight with my wife before coming to church.

Which pastor in any denomination could claim purity, could step up to the pulpit without bringing to God some brokenness? Which person in any congregation can truly come to worship without sin in his or her life? What is so terribly wrong with having a confession as one of the first orders of business when we enter God's sanctuary? There's no need to wait until we pray the confession part in the Lord's Prayer, which can so easily get lost in a ritualistic framework.

Dennis had captured the imagination of everyone in the service. With genuine confession out of the way, with buckets of grace now permeating the room, a service of joy and celebration followed. My sermon on Jesus stilling the storms in our lives couldn't have had a better introduction. There was power and change that morning. Dennis became what Henri J. M. Nouwen called the "wounded healer."

> To announce . . . that the Liberator is sitting among the poor and that the wounds are signs of hope and that today is the day of liberation, is a step very few can take. But this is exactly the announcement of the wounded healer: "The master is coming—not tomorrow, but today, not next year, but this year, not after all our misery is passed, but in the middle of it, not in another place but right here where we are standing."[16]

It was this type of honesty in worship that captivated Wes Bergen, a master's-level university student from a middle-class background. The following is an excerpt from a sermon he delivered at Welcome Inn some years later on Palm Sunday:

> Most communities are filled with wounded people who are lonely, confused, anxious. But wounds are usually covered up or left at home; we need to pretend everything is okay.
>
> I came to Welcome Inn as a wounded person, and I brought this tradition of covering up my wounds with me. Dress well, smile, and be willing to help, pretend everything is fine. But people here didn't follow these rules. Some sure did, but enough of you came as you were, and forced me to deal with you as complete but wounded people. I found it increasingly difficult to keep my own wounds inside, difficult and also unnecessary. I found that "getting ready" for church had more to do with my heart than my hair.
>
> Some of you might think it's easy and natural to come to Welcome Inn. Not so for me. I'd shower, eat breakfast, change, and find my guitar. I would get to the door and realize that I might be ready for lunch with friends, but I sure was not ready for spiritual warfare.
>
> And that's what we do here. We battle spirits of depression, alcoholism, abuse, uncaring, love of money, think-but-don't-feel pride. I confront these spirits when I come here, and sometimes there isn't enough coffee to get me ready.
>
> But ultimately there's nothing more important that Welcome Inn can do. There was healing here that I will never find anywhere else. I came because you wouldn't let me hide my wounds, because you exposed them to me.
>
> And that is the most wonderful, life-giving, yet bitterly difficult thing anyone can do. I want to thank you from the bottom of my heart. . . . I came here a wounded person and you showed me the love of God.[17]

The Torn Bulletin

I was proud of a worship bulletin I had put together announcing our summer camping program in which hundreds of youngsters and older persons would participate. Albert, one of our volunteer photographers, had taken an amazing picture the previous year, precisely when one of the boys had blown the water apart after jumping from the popular rope swing at camp. I had managed to get this onto the bulletin with the words, "Are you ready for the summer splash?"

As worship began, I looked out the window and noticed Tommy, who was about nine, sitting quietly on a swing in the center's play area with his head drooping. I went outside and invited him to join us, calling him from a distance, but received no response. As I bent down and patiently tried to talk to him, he finally stuttered, "I've . . . got . . . no . . . friends, not even Jonathan," our youngest son, who was his age. "He . . . will . . . never . . . want to be my friend."

I grabbed the adjoining swing and sat with him. His mom suffered from severe depression and was at times unable to take care of even the basic necessities of life. A few days earlier I had been called to his home because his parents were fighting. It was after midnight, and his dad was physically trying to keep his mom from walking out into the darkness. I was grateful that eventually calm was restored and a measure of reconciliation had occurred.

Tommy followed me into church, and I gave him the bul-

letin on which I had worked so hard. I thought it might enter-
tain him if he got bored. He gradually settled into his chair and
I began to concentrate on worship. When I checked on him
after a few moments, I saw him take the bulletin, deliberately
tear it in half, crumple it, and throw it on the floor. My anger
quickly surfaced.

"So much for my creativity," I mused with chagrin. I struggled to let go of my emotions and pondered what it would take
to help the boy.

Doreen was giving the message that morning. She finished
her comments and opened the floor for our usual sermon talk-
back. I hadn't heard much of the message, but I knew it was
on the feeding of the five thousand (Matthew 14:13-21).

Lillian, who lived on a small pension, immediately sprang
up and said she was running home to get some frozen fish.
"My friend caught oodles of fish up north and last night I
filled up my freezer. I want to share my good fortune with all
of you. Wait, I'll be back in ten minutes."

I saw Tommy perk up. He didn't mind waiting. When
Lillian returned, he was first in line. With beaming, brown
eyes and a generous grin, he waved good-bye to me and said,
"My parents both like fish and there's not much food in the
house." Lifting his two fish in the air as he ran down the street,
he cheerfully called out, "This will make them happy!"

The miracle of feeding the five thousand had been spoken
and had happened again in one of our North American cities.
The torn bulletin now was a non-issue. The fire gushed inside
us. To God be the glory!

But are there not more fish to share? Are there more kingdom surprises waiting for us? As we ate our noon meal of
plenty that day, there was much food for heart and mind and
soul.

A Pause in the Action

Within a week two people actively involved at the center had died suddenly.

Gord died when he went back into a fire to rescue his pregnant daughter. He managed to push her out of the second-story window onto a narrow ledge before he succumbed to the black smoke. Only a few days later, John, who had become the friendly volunteer driver for the center's van, died in a car crash attributed to an aneurysm. Both men were relatively young and left behind grieving families with children. The community was devastated.

In memory of those two Welcome Inn friends, North Enders rallied to set up an endowment fund for people in need. The name of the fund quickly caught on after it was suggested by a gifted local musician who with her husband had experienced periods of unemployment: the From the Heart Fund. A special evening of original poetry, songs, and artistic pieces had already raised a significant amount.

A Sunday was set aside as a fundraising day combined with a service of remembrance. The church was full. Some people sat on the stairway at the back of the sanctuary that led to an upstairs office. As the offering containers were passed around, many generously gave of their limited resources. Our practice was to place the gathered gifts on the front table, after which someone from the congregation would lead a blessing.

During the prayer I noticed Murray getting very upset. We

all loved Murray, and though his talk was little more than a grunt, we thought of him not as someone with disabilities, but as someone with a contribution to make. The prayer was barely finished when Murray's unmistakably guttural sounds filled the room, and we saw him pointing at Sean, one of the rowdy teenagers sitting in the front row.

"What's wrong, Murray?" I anxiously whispered. "What's bothering you?"

With that invitation, he stood up and took a step toward Sean. He continued aiming his index finger toward Sean, and in a firm, accusatory manner, uttered a language that could not be deciphered. By then there was one of those necessary but interesting pauses in worship that can only happen in a place where that kind of honest freedom is permitted. Sean was growing increasingly uncomfortable.

Had Murray had some kind of fight with this young fellow, perhaps before the service? Had Sean picked on him?

Then Murray began to point intermittently to the offering bag. I noticed that the neatness of the table had been disturbed and a bill was loosely dangling from the cloth collection container. It suddenly occurred to me: Had Sean taken something out of the offering during the prayer while all, or nearly all, eyes were closed?

Right there I asked Sean what this meant. "Did you take something that doesn't belong to you?" With Murray pointing to his pockets and the entire assembly looking at him, Sean was no longer able to protect himself. He got up, went to the offering bag, and emptied his pockets of the stolen money. The congregation cheered and the worship service continued.

Later one of the VSers came to me and excitedly commented, "I'm so glad to be part of this church. I feel so warm inside, and I get goose pimples all over me. Isn't it surprising how it seems like every day new, unexpected gifts within people keep emerging?"

"That is Christian community at its best," I said.

Easter Replaces Good Friday

It was always good to come home after much activity at the center. One spring evening I had our four youngsters all wanting to participate in making supper. It was a challenge, but I managed to give each one a job, although two of them left to play before I could adequately supervise them. Doreen finally arrived after a late-afternoon meeting, and we had supper together. For a change we were all home, so the evening was taken up with practicing piano, watching a program on TV, homework for the older ones, and story time. Finally the boys were fast asleep, and after a quick devotional, we also lay down our weary bodies and slept.

Suddenly, the phone jarred us out of our tranquility. I grabbed the receiver and an anxious voice yelled, "Come over quick! Joey's gone crazy. He's mad. It's hell around here. We need you. Will you come?"

We love our sleep, but this request was obviously urgent. Within seconds we had decided that I would go to the second-floor rooming house above some commercial outlets where Erin and Jim and their emotionally challenged sixteen-year-old son lived.

It was Doreen's turn to stay home with the kids, but she was wide-awake and would be praying for me. I was going into a crisis situation, and we both knew there was danger involved.

For years Joey had been treated for emotional as well as physical problems. Although Erin wanted to love her son, she had a hard time breaking through the crust of abuse she herself had suffered. Her scars manifested themselves in an uncultured wall of resistance that could be penetrated only through patient, graceful, Spirit-led listening. Even then it often seemed impossible. Jim had only recently come into the picture.

Joey had been placed in numerous foster homes and treatment centers, but none had handled him satisfactorily. More recently he had come to live at home, but there had been a serious question whether the apparent stability in his life would last.

When I walked up the creaking steps to the second floor and saw a huge gash in the door to the apartment, I realized that this would be more challenging than the crises I usually encountered. I felt strangely confident.

"Come on in," I heard Erin yell in a panicked voice. Carefully I opened the door and moved into the dimly lit room. As my eyes began to focus, I froze in my tracks. I had entered into a Good Friday scene. Violence surrounded me; the air was thick with hostility. The fridge had been tipped upsidedown, its door half-open and the contents oozing into the room. Broken dishes were scattered everywhere. In one corner, cowering against the wall were Erin and Jim, yelling obscenities and trying to protect themselves, their hands in front of their faces. On the other side of the room, Joey lunged forward with a butcher knife in his hand, waving it back and forth, threatening to kill his stepfather.

I was in the middle. Foolishly, Jim hurled cutting insults across the room back to Joey. Erin, in her raspy voice, also heaped confronting blame upon blame on her son.

In a split second, hundreds of thoughts flashed through my mind. I knew I could easily become the target of the rage bursting out around me. My own mortality distracted me: Who will take care of my children? What about Doreen? How can I protect myself? (As I write this, I'm shivering all over, reliving the terror of those moments.) If I made a move toward the door to escape, Joey would be after me in a second. I could not retreat from the dagger-like look in Joey's eyes that said, "Don't you try to move."

I was open and vulnerable to Good Friday violence. And didn't Jesus say on the cross, "Father into your hands I commit my Spirit"? God was my only hope.

I took a deep breath that was more than a physical inhaling, and an amazing thing happened. An overwhelming calmness filled me, and my initial fear disappeared. The power of the resurrection entered the scene of violence.

Very gently but firmly I repeatedly said to Joey, "You know where the knife belongs. Joey, you know where the knife belongs. Joey, you know where the knife belongs."

In front of me was one of those rectangular tables with a cutlery drawer. It was from the now partially open drawer that Joey had grabbed the knife. Slowly and gently, without moving my body and keeping my eyes fixed on Joey, I gradually lowered one hand until I touched the drawer. I cautiously opened it a bit further. Instinctively, or better said, with the Spirit's mysterious prompting, I knew that any hint of aggressiveness on my part could very easily trigger an act of violence. All the while, I kept repeating those words: "Joey, you know where the knife belongs."

Very slowly Joey began to inch his way toward me, flashing the knife in front of him. I could see Jim and Erin's concern for me. The cursing had diminished and the attention was now squarely focused on me and Joey.

Deep within me, I knew the power of Easter was present. Truth, love, faith, and peace, all that the risen Christ stands for, infiltrated the explosive furor in the room. Joey's quivering hand held the knife just a few inches from my body. What was he going to do? Would he use the knife? Would the spirit of Peace prevail? By the grace of God I was able to stand quietly beside the table. With a burst of decisive energy, he thrust the knife into the drawer, and with a big inward sigh of relief, I closed it gently—ever so gently.

Joey was slowly coming to his senses and seemed to realize what could have happened. There was a silence, broken by Jim's own style of confession, "We need to all get along."

There was more disarmament work to be done. A number of homemade weapons had to be dismantled. Joey took me to his bedroom. Stashed under his bed was a long pipe on which he had duct-taped a large knife, to use as a spear. From there he led me to another corner of the house where he had strategically placed another of his homemade implements of destruction. Firmly and lovingly, I asked Joey to destroy every one of the weapons. He was the one who had made them and needed to take that responsibility.

Easter replaced Good Friday in that apartment. I had been at the tomb, experienced the risen Christ, and become an agent helping bring peace into a volatile situation. Erin and Jim too were beginning to experience the joy of the resurrection in that turbulent apartment.

I don't know where Joey is today, but a few years later, while pastoring in another city, I received an ecstatic call from Erin. "I'm getting baptized tomorrow, I'm so excited." I remembered how she had once taken pleasure in arguing profusely in small groups, "There is no Lord." I smiled and gave thanks to God, and again celebrated the power of Easter with a prayer that people everywhere would claim this accessible gift.

Peace Be with You

Right next door to us lived Brian, Thelma, and Thelma's eight-year-old-son. Brian had come into the picture less than a year earlier. Soon after they moved into the rental property, we became aware of the severe marriage problems this couple was having. A radiant courtship had quickly degenerated into a marriage that was anything but beautiful. Our tall, two-story, brick houses were only a few feet apart, their dining room and kitchen facing ours.

At meals, we often winced as we witnessed the fighting and abuse. Once Thelma became so angry that she threw a glass jar at Brian. It missed him but shattered their large picture window right in front of us.

Alcoholism increasingly took hold of Brian. Sometimes he came home late in the evening, driving his car too fast for the narrow driveway between our houses. The sudden jolt of his vehicle as it grazed our house sometimes woke us at night. His hostility and belligerence caused us to fear what he might do next.

From the start, we felt God had placed this family into our lives, so we did all we could to befriend them. We invited them for coffee and readily accepted invitations to their house, where they always treated us with genuine hospitality. Their son got along well with our second youngest.

When Brian was sober, we could have congenial conversations, and he was always ready to lend a hand with a project in the house. When he drank, however, Brian was unpredictable. I felt helpless when once he grabbed me so hard that I had marks on my wrist for a few days. A burgeoning anger was beginning to be directed beyond his family, and ironically, toward his closest friends. We sheltered his wife from abuse on several occasions, and soon we seemed to be on his "list."

After one particularly violent episode, Thelma came over to call the police. When all seemed settled again, Brian agreed to leave the house, and we thought we could breathe again. We had just gone to bed when the phone rang. It was Brian's sister. In a hoarse whisper she warned, "Brian's at my house. He says he's got a gun in the back of his car and he's coming your way. He says he's got three bullets, 'for you-know-who.' "

Our peace evaporated. We trembled, afraid for our kids, afraid for ourselves. We expected at any moment to hear the scraping of metal on bricks as Brian's car charged up the driveway. Our doors were locked, but we felt little security. Not only could the aging cedar be easily kicked in, but several large windows at ground level provided little deterrence for someone intent on entering the house. We hugged one another and prayed harder than ever before.

We called the police, who came to talk to us. They were pleasant and professional, and tried to alleviate our fears, but they said they were powerless to take action unless Brian actually did something. "But that would be too late," we pleaded. They stayed as long as they could, but soon left for other calls. We were alone again, with only those inadequate doors and windows to protect us.

Our spirits seemed to be locked up tightly and our sense of security shattered by the powerful drive of fear. Yes, we wanted to trust God, but we still trembled most of the night. In some measure we identified with the band of frightened disciples after the crucifixion of Jesus (John 20:19-23). They were in a crisis, fearing for their lives, and huddled together behind securely fastened doors. Their best friend and mentor, with whom they'd had "coffee" many times before, had brutally been murdered by those who opposed all that he stood for. They too were potential targets.

As he did for them, Jesus came into our midst, as it were, and said, "Peace be with you." And then we heard those same words a second time, third time, and practically all night. Our spirits gradually became calm and we knew that we were not alone. God was with us.

Brian didn't show up. We were protected during that night of uncertainty. Someone blocked his path and muzzled his gun. Doreen and I knew who that Someone was. Our Protector was at hand.

The next day we had agreed to host a denominational worker in our home. When he heard our story, our voices still trembling, he recognized that we needed a break from our situation. "You need rest and renewal that will help you to cope with the stresses you are facing," he said. Quickly he arranged for Doreen and me to attend a church workers' retreat at Wellspring in Maryland, which was about to begin.

"I had thought of inviting you in the first place," he said. Before the day was over, the kids were in the care of friends and we were on our way.

A retreat was the best gift anyone could have given us. We still talk about the quiet, lovely setting and the crimson, yellow, and orange fall foliage that welcomed us. It was our first silent retreat; we were instructed after supper to talk to no one for the next twenty-four hours.

Our resources began to be replenished during this time of centering with the Holy One. By the time we drove home again, we held a strength and confidence that can only be explained as the mystery of having walked with Jesus. After we returned, we discovered that Brian was moving out of the neighborhood and leaving his troubled marriage. Of course, we were immensely relieved. Peace and gladness had once again returned to our lives.

The Stranger's Face

Joyce Lichtenberger's daughter Candice had come to our vacation Bible school and loved it. Joyce and her husband, Perry, noticed the positive values with which their daughter came home. But what brought the couple to the congregation was their experience at the closing program.

During the week, about a dozen adults, mostly parents of the children, met daily to talk about human sexuality. "If in a church you can talk about something as pertinent to life as sex, I'd like to be there," Joyce had said.

We heard that Joyce and her husband had musical abilities and had performed in bars and nightclubs. So Doreen invited her to check out some of the songs we had in our repertoire and sing one in a service shortly after Easter. The worship centered on the story of the disciples who failed to recognize Jesus on the road to Emmaus after the resurrection (Luke 24:13-35). Joyce surprised us when she wrote and sang her own song:

The Stranger's Face

With pain they cried as they walked on by
    And the stranger walked beside,
They have taken all we held so dear,
    Our freedom crucified.
And the Stranger spoke of promises
    That the prophets said were true.

Don't stop believing, you're salvation's come;
   What's been done's been done for you.

   And the Stranger was so loving.
   And the Stranger was so kind.
   And wasn't it like a fire burning?
   Could the Lord be far behind?

And in my memories I see a young man
   Wearing faded old blue jeans,
His long hair falling as he held a young girl
   With, oh, so faded dreams.
I remember how he listened,
   And how the women softly cried,
And how I thought he looked like Jesus,
   And how we felt the fire inside.

   And the Stranger was so loving.
   And the Stranger was so kind.
   And wasn't it like a fire burning?
   Could the Lord be far behind?

In the world we find the lonely;
   Hungry people filled with doubt;
A man lends a hand doing all he can;
   One more stranger reaching out.
A man is lonely, sleeps on a doorway;
   It's a trap with no way out.
Along comes another, calls him his brother;
   Together they find their way out.

   And the Stranger was so loving.
   And the Stranger was so kind.
   And wasn't it like a fire burning?
   Could the Lord be far behind?

When you feel the love of another come
　Like warm sunshine in the night
And you feel the chain of bondage fall,
　And wings have taken flight,
Or you see the smile of a happy child
　Or the miracles in space,
Just close your eyes and you'll recognize
　The familiar Stranger's face.

　And the Stranger was so loving.
　And the Stranger was so kind.
　And wasn't it like a fire burning?
　Could the Lord be far behind?[18]

What Joyce captured so powerfully in this song is the coherence of biblical material and human experience. She began by telling the story in the Scriptures, where there was interaction with, but no recognition of, Jesus. In the disciples' disappointment, the stranger was encouraging, bringing hope to the conversation: "Don't stop believing."

In the second stanza Joyce remembered a childhood experience (which she shared more completely with the congregation) of being the "young girl with, oh, so faded dreams." She and her mother, the "women [who] softly cried," were homeless. To escape their problems her mother used up the last of her money for the trip, but they were stranded, miles from home and sitting on the front steps of a lonely bus station out in the country. Both were in tears with nowhere to go when a caring young man "wearing faded old blue jeans," with all the scars of a street person, appeared like an angel, out of nowhere. He identified with their plight and gave them food and bus tickets to a place in another city, where her mother could get help. Joyce recognized this unlikely good Samaritan with the long, scraggly hair, as Jesus, and reflected on the "fire burning" inside of her.

In stanza three she placed the biblical story into the reality of our day and of the increasing homeless population. She didn't dwell on the plight of those who are poor, but articulated the gifts of the homeless, as "a man lends a hand" and "together they find their way" out of the trap of poverty.

In the final stanzas, she brings the story to whatever we've experienced—the "sunshine, . . . the smile of a happy child"—and asks us to pause: "Just close your eyes and you'll recognize the familiar Stranger's face."

The chorus speaks of the fire burning inside us when the Great One is near, whether we recognize God or not.

–6–
Lead Me to a New Tomorrow

Say to those who are of a fearful heart,
"Be strong, do not fear!"

Then the eyes of the blind shall be opened,
And the ears of the deaf unstopped;
then the lame shall leap like a deer, and
the tongue of the speechless sing for joy.
(Isaiah 35:4a, 5-6a)

There's enough for everyone. There's so much greed.
If you share, there's hope.
—A North Ender on a disability pension

I have been blessed with people who call me "sister" and those
that call me "brother." I have shared my sandwich with a
stranger and accept the same kindness when I am in need.
God's love and the kindness of spirit of his children are very
much alive, and are more than ever surrounding each and
every one of us. Peace is what we all strive for, and love is what
will save us.
—Joyce Lichtenberger, July 2005

The North End Parable Challenge

There was a country with an abundance of natural resources that were the envy of the entire world. Unfortunately, in that same country were poor folk, as well as plenty of rich, and they each tended to keep to their kind of people. The well-to-do were the ones who called the shots—economically, religiously, and culturally—in that society. They were the ones who benefited the most from the political and social structures that had become enshrined in its fabric. Indeed, the wealthy were becoming wealthier, while the poor tended to stay the same, or even fall further behind.

It was with some reluctance that the rich supported a system set up by the government for helping the poor. It allowed officials to hand out to the poor a small portion of their annual budget. When it came to set that budget, the needs of the poor were generally the last to be considered. In time, the poor became mere recipients, and the system created an unhealthy, dependent relationship. Poverty became cyclical in nature and continued year after year. The relationship was one in which the poor became economically, socially, and politically *dependent* on the well-to-do.

A second wealthy country also had rich and poor people. It also had a welfare system that reinforced a poverty trap from which few were able to escape. Some of the poor and some of the rich saw that this generation-after-generation dependence was harmful and decided that the best way to solve the dilemma was to form two separate, *independent* groups of people, each managing their own resources. The country's wealth was divided exactly equally and resulted in the establishment of new national boundaries. The two people groups lived apart, with no sharing and no interaction between them. But each group soon found itself missing important skills and talents needed to sustain a growing community. Both groups suffered, but were too proud to change the arrangement.

In a third country, similar to the first in its division of resources and population, the poor became so frustrated that they wanted a revolution to remove the injustice in their society. Many used violence as they lashed out at political leaders. Subsequently, the people of power set up new laws, built more jails, and many of the poor found themselves becoming even more bitter. No one seemed to understand what they were fighting for. Some of the poor internalized their frustrations, punishing their own families and even people who were trying to help them. This *counterdependent* relationship between rich and poor set up a negative spiral; violence and terror became widespread.

There was a fourth country where voices from both sides began declaring that something is wrong when the rich and the poor either avoid or fight each other. They realized it wasn't helpful to have a system in which one group is so dependent on the other, year after year. They wanted to make changes but knew they had to work at them together.

And so began a political, social, and economic movement that changed both the fabric of society and the lives of individuals. People out of work found jobs. The disabled began to make as decent a living as other people. Some living in expensive neighborhoods soon lived side by side with those who had little. Some who'd been on welfare shared decision making in corporate boardrooms. Employers sought the talents and skills of all income groups. Guidelines for welfare and subsidies to corporations were revamped to reflect fairness and opportunity for all.

Many could be heard to say, "We have a common ancestry, we are inextricably woven together, and we have a common future." The rich brought their gifts of planning and management, while the poor emphasized sharing, relaxation, and claiming the beauty of the present. With so much goodwill, there was enough for all and much joy in this country. The relationship between those who were poor and those who were rich could only be characterized as *interdependent*.

And suddenly, within this country, spiritual renewal in its fullest sense took place. One Sunday morning these words of Jesus were read in church: "The Spirit of the Lord is upon me, because he has appointed me to bring good news to the poor" (Luke 4:18a). Everyone knew that this prophecy was being fulfilled right in their midst.

I Should Have Taken It Off the Rack

It was my turn to work in the ecumenical clothing room set up in one of the local churches. Clothing was given away for whatever sum people could afford, or it was free to anyone who didn't have even a quarter. I had come early to scout the newly donated items. Would there perhaps be something I could use? It was the unofficial understanding that a volunteer could take home one piece of clothing for the time spent managing the room.

Although wearing a suit was never a pleasure to me, I still needed one for formal occasions. Being a tall, slim guy, it was always hard for me to find the right size. I hardly expected to find something, but tried on every suit that day and was surprised to come up with a treasure. It fit perfectly, and I liked the blackness, the texture, and the subtle pinstripes. "I'll claim it for myself," I thought.

Just then my first customer arrived, so I quickly draped the suit under a large women's coat, thinking it would be unseen there. I knew Jack, a friendly, congenial man who was ever ready to strike up a conversation. He was always on the go, on the road to somewhere. It would be unusual not to spy him at some point in the week, crisscrossing the North End.

Often Jack knocked on doors of businesses and offered to run errands, or do odd jobs. Those efforts would give him a few dollars to supplement his meager disability check. When he couldn't find work, he got groceries from food banks and churches to support his wife and three children. Once I saw him using only grocery carts to move the entire contents of his house about five blocks to a "new" one.

Jack was at the clothing room to look for a suit for a wedding, he told me. I tried to avoid showing him my "claimed" suit. "Nothing seems to fit," he said. "I need something for Saturday. I can't just show up in these old grubbies."

Disgusted after trying on every possible combination, Jack started walking down the steps to the front entrance. My feelings vacillated between my self-interest and my conscience. My chest pounded. Why hadn't I just taken the suit off the rack and placed it with my belongings? Then the transaction would have been complete and legitimate.

Just at the last minute, I hollered down the stairs. "Wait, there seems to be just one more here for you to try on." Somewhat reluctantly, Jack came back up the narrow staircase. "I don't know if this color and pattern will suit you," I dishonestly remarked.

The jacket fit perfectly. Jack was delighted.

"But what if the pants don't fit," I hedged. "You're not going to like it." They were actually much too loose on him. But when Jack said his sister-in-law would take them in, he took away any hope of my claim to the treasure. He gave the kitty a few dollars for his prized possession and happily trotted down the stairs.

Driven by a guilty conscience, I reflected on my experience of the morning. There I was, strong and healthy, relatively well-to-do, with an education, a job, and a bank account. My extended family often brought us free food from their Niagara farm, we had a large freezer full of food that could last us for many months, and my clothes closet was jammed to capacity. I had hoarded, and almost stolen, a suit from my friend on the street. How well I fit with those in a privileged positions in our society, who tend to store up all kinds of treasures for ourselves while those living below the poverty line dream of more equal access to resources and cry out for justice.

The material goods to which the wealthy readily have access are quickly defined as a personal and God-given natural right: an abundant amount of designer clothing, the latest computer technology, books and education, vacation cruises and resorts, concerts, music lessons, entertainment centers, and much more. To my mind came a sermon I once heard from a fiery African-American preacher, who put it this way: "It will take just as much of a miracle today to persuade the rich to share with those who are poor in our cities as it took for five thousand hungry people to be fed by five loaves and two fish many years ago."

A Surprise Critique of My Own Giving

Everyone in the small congregation that emerged at the center loved Andrea. She was intellectually and socially challenged and needed a trustee to manage her disability check. It was awkward to talk with her because her speech was somewhat limited, but everyone delighted in her wide, beautiful, gracious smile.

One Sunday I sat next to Andrea while Doreen led worship. I heard how Andrea enjoyed with her full voice every note in the songs of praise we were singing. Each note was way off tune, each word garbled.

Her joy caused me to contemplate how I would respond in worship if I were disabled the way Andrea is. What if I required a van to pick me up every Sunday from an over-priced, profit-driven lodging home and bring me to a faith community where the moment I entered the door I would be greeted with warm hellos? What would it be like to be in her shoes?

It took me awhile to get over thinking that everyone needed to be "churchly correct," especially as far as singing went. But eventually I began to concentrate on God's presence with us. The atmosphere in the church deeply moved me to a profound Pentecost experience, where solidarity and unity of singing in tongues existed among Andrea, myself, the congregation, and the almighty Creator God.

But what moved the experience to an even higher plane

was the offering time. I couldn't help but notice Andrea desperately searching every corner of her shiny black purse. Then, finding her lost coin at last, she held it, observed it from all sides, and with a wonderfully big smile carefully dropped one copper penny into the offering bag. As an amen to her worship action, and with an expression of deep satisfaction and joy, she quietly folded her hands, giving God the glory.

"Didn't Jesus say something about this kind of giving?" I pondered. Our family tithed and gave our 10 percent. And there was much more money left in our bank account. Oh, and there was the income tax refund Doreen and I were expecting; in our minds we had already spent it without thinking about the church. We thought we might put it into a more high-risk investment, which could pay off in the end.

Andrea had given all she had, and we were giving out of our excess. The worship Pentecost experience challenged me to a surprisingly new type of thinking that could radically alter our giving patterns. The delightful expression of joy I observed on Andrea's face as she presented her gift of a magic penny was engraved in my mind.

Isn't it striking that in the Scripture passage we've come to know as the story of the widow's mite, Jesus upheld as a new pattern for giving the example of a widow who lived below the poverty line?

Jesus spent hours trying to teach the religious leaders of his day about God's deeper principles. I have imagined how tired he must have been at the end of a day of kingdom work: He paused to rest at the entrance of the temple, perhaps with his head drooped on his hands. Beside him were thirteen trumpet-shaped offering containers, each designated for a different cause.

Jesus looked up and noticed the rich putting gifts into the boxes. I'm sure as the many large coins were tossed into the receptacles and trickled down into the box below, there was a

fair amount of clanging. People would have noticed such contributions and applauded, which is what the giver wanted.
And then Jesus observed this widow of few means putting in
the very tiniest currency of the day, two small copper coins,
worth a penny, according to the text.

We might say she could have at least kept one for herself.
But Jesus commends her to the crowd: "Truly, I tell you, this
poor widow has put in more than all of them; for all of them
have contributed out of their abundance, but she out of her
poverty has put in all she had to live on" (Luke 21:3-4).

I wonder if her name was Andrea?

Yes, We Will Have a Church

Like the biblical Abraham and Sarah, who heard the call of God to a new land, Eleanor was a person who pursued a faith journey. She grew up in a troubled family and at fifteen dropped out of school and left home. During the day she worked odd jobs, earning a few dollars here and there. Often at day's end, with nowhere to go, she landed on the street. To get a few hours of sleep, she would try the doors of parked cars until she found one unlocked.

Eleanor eventually found some security by moving in with a caring man who worked for a casket company. But the financial stability soon ended when the company went out of business and her live-in partner couldn't find other work. By this time both were experiencing health problems that prevented steady employment. With their inadequate income of unemployment insurance and later welfare, it wasn't long before they were living in substandard housing in the North End. On top of that, they discovered that their young son, the joy of their life, was developmentally challenged. They accepted him with his limitations and provided the best care they could.

It was not until Eleanor almost died of a collapsed lung that she decided to get on the journey with God. In her hospital bed, as she hovered between life and death, she "saw Jesus, as plain as day. There he was, all in white, welcoming me to join him, and I did."

As a result of this dramatic experience, she quit her excessive smoking and drinking and began to participate actively in the growing faith community at the center. Soon she was baptized and married the man she had lived with for more than twenty years. She was often the informal spokesperson for the congregation, especially when new people came to visit or there was a congregational exchange. Her ability to speak without notes and candidly talk about her daily life with God, as well as about her struggles with poverty, captivated many a group. The scars of poverty were present in Eleanor, but so was her flaming passion for God.

This was at a time when the programs at the center and the church were expanding rapidly. We still met in the large house with a walkout basement. But it seemed we were always renovating and taking out walls for the ever-increasing number of people who used the facilities. One day Doreen and I counted over 120 people in the main room. I shuddered at what the fire marshal might say.

But there was very little money available. The center's board did some fundraising, but there was barely enough to cover ongoing expenses. The growing faith community had few in it who were not living on some form of assistance. Finding adequate rental space or a building to purchase seemed out of the question after urban renewal had taken most of the larger buildings in the area. Most people saw little hope of a solution to our space constraints. I was usually one of the optimistic ones, but at this time I had little faith.

During worship that day, about seventy people had gathered in the low-ceilinged, green-carpeted room. Eleanor got up and said she had something to share. Making her way to the front of the semicircle of friends, she spoke with conviction. "I've been dreaming about a new church building for us. It's not only a dream; it's going to be a reality. I know we are going to get it. It's going to have a cross and will be inviting for everyone. No one will be excluded. God is good, and God will remember us."

She told us how she had followed that vision to a vacant North End lot at the corner of Burlington Street and James Street. She had taken a rock and placed it as an altar at the center of the lot, and then had prayed, she said, as Abraham and Sarah had prayed: "God, give us a church building right here."

Eleanor wanted everyone to know that our space needs would be met. Not all of us were convinced. Rarely, however, have I witnessed such powerfully simplistic and profound faith, expressed in such a convincing manner, against all odds. When the congregation sang the sending song, "We shall go out with joy," over and over, then faster and faster, the momentum was so great that the exuberant singing continued even after a string on the accompanist's guitar snapped. After the service, the optimism and enthusiasm spilled out into the North End. Despite my skepticism, I couldn't help but be swept up in the joy that our prophetic Eleanor had released.

Less than a month later we received a letter that said the Baptist Church a block-and-a-half from the empty lot would soon be available. It was even closer to our present location, and for an unusually low price we could initially rent it with an option of purchase after one year. Would we be interested? It seemed unbelievable! In a remarkably short time we were in the building, which became the permanent home of the center and the church.

Ironically, but perhaps with some symbolism attached, the first funeral actually held in the new building was Eleanor's, more than ten years later.

In the letter to the Hebrews, the author identified numerous faith heroes, giving particular attention to Abraham and Sarah. If that writer were penning his words today, we know someone else who would be on the list.

My Psalm of Praise Receives a Corrective

Bless the LORD, O my soul,
    and all that is within me,
    bless his holy name.
Bless the LORD, O my soul,
    and do not forget all his benefits—
who forgives all your iniquity,
    who heals all your diseases,
who redeems your life from the Pit,
    who crowns you with steadfast love and mercy,
who satisfies you with good as long as you live
    so that your youth is renewed like the eagle's.

The LORD works vindication and justice
    for all who are oppressed.
He made known his ways to Moses,
    his acts to the people of Israel.
The LORD is merciful and gracious,
    slow to angry and abounding in steadfast love.
He will not always accuse,
    nor will he keep his anger forever.
He does not deal with us according to our sins,
    nor repay us according to our iniquities.
For as the heavens are high above the earth,
    so great is his steadfast love toward those
        who fear him;

as far as the east is from the west,
  so far he removes our transgressions from us.
As a father has compassion for his children,
  so the LORD has compassion for those who fear him.
For he knows how we are made;
  he remembers that we are dust.

As for mortals, their days are like grass;
  they flourish like a flower of the field;
for the wind passes over it, and it is gone,
  and its place knows it no more.
But the steadfast love of the Lord is from everlasting
to everlasting
  on those who fear him,
  and his righteousness to children's children,
to those who keep his covenant and remember to do
his commandments.

The LORD has established his throne in the heavens,
  and his kingdom rules over all.
Bless the LORD, O you his angels,
  you mighty ones who do his bidding,
    obedient to his spoken word.
Bless the LORD, all his hosts,
  his ministers that do his will.
Bless the LORD, all his works,
  in all places of his dominion.
Bless the LORD, O my soul! (Psalm 103)

I had grown up with this psalm, the great poetic expression of the young shepherd boy, David. I imagined him playing his harp high on the hillsides, overlooking the lush valley below, the sheep quietly grazing. This was the psalm my parents had tried to have me memorize, but I had failed miserably from the middle of the second verse on. Yet I noted something majestic in the words.

As a teenager I recognized that Psalm 103 was often used at silver and golden wedding anniversaries and special celebratory services in my congregation. In grade ten my memorization skills were again put to the test. In the private Christian school I was attending I was forced to commit to memory the first thirteen verses, because not to memorize them would mean to remain standing. The teacher would select us one by one at random, and we would then each need to repeat the subsequent verse. If we failed, we would be punished by not being able to sit for the rest of the period. It was agony, but I finally learned the lines.

Facetiously, at the end of one session, I blurted out in class that we had missed the best part of the psalm, the last section (I hadn't really thought of the content). My teacher wasn't impressed with the wisecrack and gave me a stern lecture.

I had memorized almost two-thirds of the psalm, but if I were asked to summarize the contents, I would have declared it to be solely a psalm of praise.

Years later, Doreen and I and several VSers were together in a group of a dozen people, most of whom hadn't grown up in the church and were reading the Bible for the first time. We looked at this psalm to help us think about God's goodness. The psalm is an elegant expression of a powerful God, but our friends came up with important themes I had completely overlooked all those years.

Someone asked why the writer felt we were like grass. "Are we not much more important to God that that?"

"Well, it's true that we're all going to die and go back to dirt at some point," one person reflected.

Others talked about the tragedies in their lives: a brother who had been run over by a train; a mother who had died young of cancer; a friend who had burned to death when the fat in her frying pan caught fire while she was making French fries. One person who had experienced a recent death said, "These people are gone from us now, but I just know we'll see them again. It does talk about God's steadfast love continuing forever. I see it here, right in verse seventeen."

In my traditional observations I had completely skipped the part about human mortality.

But the part of the Psalm that received the most attention was verse six: "The LORD works vindication and justice for all the oppressed."

"We are the oppressed," said one participant, "and these verses are good news for us. We're always running out of money because we have so little. God does not intend it to be that way. God wants all of us to have enough food and clothing and gas money so we can live comfortably, like other folks do."

One person, who had recently claimed God in her life, spoke up. "Surely, this psalm of praise is confronting to the rich." Doreen and I found ourselves getting just a little bit uncomfortable. Certainly we were rich in comparison with most others in the group. But I was shocked to realize how I had missed another major component. It was humbling as new Christians and seekers living below the poverty line brought fresh insights about this psalm. What would happen if the anniversary services using Psalm 103 took the complete picture into account? Would some of those celebrations become times when a redistribution of wealth could occur? Could those who have recreational vehicles in addition to two family cars offer a used vehicle to someone who desperately needs one? Would those who have cottages or vacation condos offer to help someone who is homeless?

And what might happen when the line between those who are rich and those who are poor becomes blurred, when we become part of the same church and we all begin reading and interpreting Scripture together? Would the justice component of the gospel message be seen as God's intention for humanity? Might a new realization emerge that God has a special concern for those who are poor, knowing they are so often without?

I Dream of a World Where There's Love in the Air

There was an anxious call from Lorena.

"Come and pick up the guns. I need them out of the house right now."

"But it's ten o'clock at night," I gently protested. "I'll come first thing in the morning."

"But my boys might pull the trigger. I'm so afraid. They're getting out of control, and if Bill comes back, there's no telling what they'll do."

I finally realized the seriousness of the situation. Without getting all the details, I imagined all kinds of scenarios. I told Lorena that Doreen and I would be over in ten minutes.

There had been numerous crises in Lorena's life in the past year, beginning with the sudden death of her husband in a car crash. The grief only compounded the mental-health issues with which she had struggled for many years. Without their father's discipline, Lorena's two teenage boys began skipping school and getting into the drug scene.

About a week before her call, we had been summoned because she feared that Bill, her brother newly released from prison, would hurt her. Bill had a major psychiatric illness and had been incarcerated because of his violence. As we tried to be a presence to Lorena that night, Bill forced his way into the house. I was able to persuade him to leave, but not before he had punched me in the chest. I felt that bruise for days.

I relived that moment of fear as I thought of the unpredictable, aggressive behavior that could emerge from her brother. I thought of Lorena, who lived with that threat day and night. I also thought of her two teenagers, who had difficulty sorting out their lives. The volatile, problematic home situation was almost too much for anyone to bear.

But then I remembered a poem Lorena had written and shared with Welcome Inn friends just a few weeks earlier:

There is Hope

Is there hope for me?
I wonder how that could be.

In my world spinning round and round,
I wonder how that might be found.

Then I remembered not to give up hope:
That's the only way a person can cope.

And all of a sudden it happened to me:
My world stopped spinning, and then I was free.

Somehow, just thinking about the confidence expressed in her words gave me the courage to go to her house again. When we entered, we discovered that she was alone. The boys weren't home, and there was no sign of her brother.

"Quick, Hugo, come and get these guns. I threw away all the ammunition, but I'm still scared my boys will use these when Bill gets back. They've threatened to block Bill from ever coming this way again."

"What shall I do with them?"

"I don't care what you do with them. Just take them," she

pleaded. "I don't ever want to see them in this house again."

I took the two old shotguns and a rifle, placed them in a large garbage bag, and carried them to the trunk of our car. At home I stuffed them in a corner of our hard-to-reach attic, where they stayed for the next ten years. Bill moved away shortly afterward and the household became somewhat more peaceful.

A few years later we were working on a community drama, with many of the Welcome Inn friends involved. The play we created focused on "the tree of life" from Genesis and Revelation, the first and last books of the Bible. Projected throughout this drama that told the story of the people God had created and continues to create, was hope for a broken world. I remembered how Lorena's optimism had grown after her home had been purged of the lethal weapons. I also knew she loved to write poems and wondered if she would create a poetic piece for the drama.

In a few days Lorena brought me this poem, which captures the direction our world needs to go:

A Dream

I dream of a world where there is love in the air;
    A place of true peace, where everyone cares.
    It doesn't matter if you are rich or poor;
    Money doesn't matter there, that's for sure.

A place where we are all equal to one another;
Where we call each other a sister or brother.

This place is like a paradise for everyone to share,
Where lambs and lions lie together without a care.

This is my dream; I hope it comes true.
You see, I know God wants this for us, too.[19]

A New Tomorrow

The music program at the center and in the faith community took on some new dimensions after Joyce and her husband and their two children became involved. The enthusiastic and joyful expressions in Joyce's songs quickly inspired others to bring out their own creativity. Juan, who had hung up his guitar five years earlier and suffered from depression, suddenly offered to bring his instrument and join the worship music team. Bill, who hadn't sung in years, gained enough confidence to close worship events with his strong tenor rendition of "May the good Lord bless you and keep you." Several teens who had lost a friend in a car accident wrote a song with Joyce's mentoring, which they shared with the whole community. There was an excitement of a "new tomorrow" in the church and the center as these hidden talents began to emerge.

While God had always been part of Joyce's life, she readily acknowledged that she had not always given priority to God and the church. The more she gave of herself in her music, the more she realized the need to recommit her life to God. On a beautiful spring day, along with six others, she was baptized to express her reconfirmation to a life of following God.

Joyce never forgot her childhood poverty, her tumultuous teen years, and the more recent times of unemployment. She composed and readily shared songs that encapsulated the dreams of those who are poor. She understood those living below the poverty line and always had a big heart for them.

Her giftedness lay in prophetically integrating ordinary life experiences with what she felt Scripture portrays as God's intention for humanity.

She was invited to provide the music ministry for a large gathering of the denomination. The song she wrote and sang encouraged a refreshing way to look at life.

Freedom in Your Love

Father, lead me to a new tomorrow,
Guide me on my way;
Liberate me from the chains that bind me
To my yesterdays.
Father, bless me with the freedom
That can only come from you,
Lead my captive heart to freedom
In your love.

Father, help me pray for my oppressors,
That you might set them free.
Fill our hearts with love for one another,
And help our eyes to see
That within our hearts we're all one family,
Everyone the same;
Lead our captive hearts to freedom
In your name.

Lead us on our journey, Lord,
Into the Promised Land,
Where lambs and lions lie together,
Where we reach to take a hand.
Let me walk beside someone with many.
Let me help those who have none.
Let us be one; let us be one.

Liberation comes to those who find
Their riches in your love;
And the journey starts the moment that
We make up our minds to come.
Let us take a hand before we judge it,
Help us to be like you;
Lead our captive hearts to freedom
In your love.[20]

What is the "new tomorrow" to which Joyce's song calls us? I believe the vision summarizes the aspirations of those who are poor, with whom Joyce identifies, and all humanity.

In our world all people have a quest, sometimes very hidden, to be free from the "chains that bind" us. This imprisonment takes on various forms that restrict us from becoming the people we are designed to be. When a spiraling bitterness sets in because we have lost our long-term employment or a grudge from a strained relationship shackles our being, we know that our "yesterdays" have imprisoned us. When our self-interest keeps moving us to the almighty number-one position, we may find ourselves forming friendships only with select groups and becoming blind to the needs of those around us. As we search our souls, we know that something is not quite right. With the kind of world we live in, we become tangled up in the corporate greed that feeds so much energy into acquiring more products than we can rightly use. This impetus for sumptuous living leads to exploitation of our natural resources and creates momentum toward a society where the wealthy become wealthier, while those who are poor are left without access to the generous treasures of this world. For Joyce, freedom and salvation from the sin-dilemma comes through her request, "Father, bless me with the freedom that can only come from you."

Being created in God's image gives everyone the impulse to

seek positive and joyful human relationships. In verse two Joyce recognizes that positive quality and pleads that we might see "that within our hearts we're all one family," which expresses itself in "a love for one another." No longer do we run each other down or resort to fighting, but instead we are called to "pray for [our] oppressors." Racism and separate groupings of rich and poor do not fit into a world where the desire is to be one. However, those who exploit or foster an economic and political climate where consumerism flourishes must not be hated but rather prayed for so that God "can set them free." Authentic freedom doesn't happen until both the oppressor and the oppressed are liberated from "the chains that bind" them.

So we live in a world of hurt and pain. But where are the stories of the peaceable reign of God? They seem to be crowded out by our preoccupation with terrorism and an excessive search for personal security. The stories of our North End friends include a longing for a world where all have equal access to the resources God has given.

Deep down, the well-to-do also know that something is not right. The burdens they face of anxiety-driven illnesses, addictions, and broken relationships cause them to search for answers. In verse three, using biblical imagery of the peaceable kingdom (Isaiah 11:6), Joyce invites all to journey into the Promised Land, "where lambs and lions lie together." This holy trek is revolutionary. Everyone is invited into a relationship of mutuality, where those who are rich and those who are poor can give and receive. "Let me walk beside someone with many. Let me help those who have none. Let us be one."

In the final verse, Joyce challenges everyone to make a firm decision. She provides glimpses of the radical and life-giving teachings of Jesus in the Sermon on the Mount, including the tough one of loving one's enemies ("oppressors"), and calls for all to "make up our minds to come" and work at bringing about the peaceable reign of God. Here economic, social, and religious barriers are broken down. "We're all one family" (verse two) and we "take a hand before we judge it" (verse four). This "new tomorrow" is a place where those living above and below the poverty line will want to be together.

Conclusion

Several years ago Doreen and I were enjoying a canoe trip down the picturesque, swirling Bow River, which runs through the heart of Calgary, Alberta. The waters at the westerly edge of the city still abound with natural parkland. It was springtime and everything was bursting with new life. Fresh poplar leaves fluttered in the breeze in their characteristic way. Marsh grasses stretched out from beneath dead brush; everything was turning a vibrant spring green. The occasional sandpiper flew in front of us, coaxing us to paddle faster.

What a wonderful creation! What powerful acts of God to observe! Surely such a world would renew the spirits of two pastors on their day off—and it did.

"Look, there's a bald eagle on the tip of that tree," Doreen whispered to me, careful not to startle the stately bird.

We marveled at the gracefulness of its large body. We watched it turn its proud white head, which has forever been labeled "bald" (I think I would have called it something else).

As we got closer, we noticed a family at the base of the same tree, oblivious to the remarkable scene above them. A father was taking a picture of his wife and young daughter, with the river as a backdrop. All he saw was the flat view directly in front of him, beautiful as it was.

As our canoe passed by we called to them in a loud whisper, "Look up!" pointing to the eagle. The photo session was suspended, and the family gazed in wonder at the beauty above. With the current picking up its pace, our canoe quickly moved downstream. But before we were out of sight, we thought we heard a faint "thank you" in the distance.

Doreen and I owe much gratitude to all our North End friends, who taught us what it means to speak and live "good news to the poor." It was a gripping discovery to realize that good news to those living below the poverty line is also good news to those who live above it. I was challenged to look up from my flat and narrow slice of landscape and take in the amazing beauty and power above and around me. New insights into a person's heritage moved me to see the strengths of all people, all who've been fashioned in God's image. Again and again I was confronted with the preoccupation of my own "photo" world. But I rejoice in the discovery and the new awareness that "the North End lives" with a God who was present long before we arrived.

Notes

1. Mennonite Voluntary Service is a missional program offered by the Mennonite Church to people of all ages. Voluntary Service Workers commit themselves to an assignment of one or two years, but sometimes longer. In return for full-time service they receive free room and board, medical costs, and a small personal allowance. They usually live in community with other volunteers. Service assignments vary and can include working in day-care and community centers, providing various forms of counseling, supporting shelters for women, men, and children, procuring housing for low-income persons, assisting in church development, and facilitating advocacy and social-action activity in accordance with the teachings of Jesus.

2. Donald B. Kraybill, *The Upside-Down Kingdom* (Scottdale, Pa., and Kitchener, Ont.: Herald Press, 1978), p 21.

3. Ibid.

4. Henri J. M Nouwen, *The Return of the Prodigal Son* (New York: Doubleday, 1992), p. 105-6.

5. Voluntary Service Workers were often assigned to specific individuals with exceptional needs. Through their regular visits, special life-changing friendships were formed that went both ways.

6. "Jesus Accepts Us" by Lois Corney © 1985. Published in *Welcome Inn Community Centre and Church 1966-1986*, edited by Helen Unrau, p. 88. Lois died December 11, 1997.

7. Albert Willms, ed., *Welcome Inn—VS, Inner City Ministry* (Hamilton, Ont., 1977).

8. "I Am the One" by Shelly Lewis © 1981. Published in *Welcome Inn Community Centre and Church 1966-1986*, edited by Helen Unrau, p. 77.

9. Jean Vanier, "Welcoming Jesus in the Poor," first published in English in *The Canadian Catholic Review*, vol. 1 (Richmond Hill, Ont.: Daybreak Publications, 1983), p. 14. Male pronouns have been changed to honor Vanier's inclusive intentions.

10. Mary Jo Leddy has a passion for justice and is the founding editor of *Catholic New Times*. She has a compassion for refugees and all

those who suffer from poverty, and lives at Romero House in Toronto. A book of hers I have found particularly helpful is *At the Border Called Hope, Where Refugees Are Neighbors.*

11. Menno Simons was an early Anabaptist leader during Reformation times in the sixteenth century. He helped unite various groups in a common understanding of the Christian faith, which eventually resulted in the followers being called Mennonites. His writings bring together strong teachings on the centrality of Jesus, a voluntary commitment to Christ, the significance of the discerning community, a seven-days-a-week discipleship, and a commitment to peace, nonviolence, and loving one's enemies.

12. See Paul's representative listing of gifts in Romans 12:5-8; 1 Corinthians 12:27–13:13; Ephesians 4:11-13.

13. "Recommendations to the Provincial Social Assistance Review Committee by the Friends of Welcome Inn Living Below the Poverty Line," Hamilton, Ont., November 20, 1986.

14. Mother Teresa, *Total Surrender,* Brother Angelo Devananda, ed. (New York: Walker and Company, 1993), p. 134-5.

15. Anabaptists were one of several groups that grew out of the Protestant Reformation in the early sixteenth century. Central to their beliefs were nonresistance to violence, the separation of church and state, and the doctrine of baptism upon confession of faith.

16. Henri J. M. Nouwen, *The Wounded Healer* (New York: Doubleday, 1972), p. 95.

17. From the Welcome Inn Community Centre and Church newsletter, March 1994, p. 2.

18. "The Stranger's Face" words and music by Joyce Lichtenberger © 1987. Used by permission.

19. The poems "There is a Hope" © 1986 and "A Dream" © 1988 were written by a Welcome Inn friend whose pseudonym in this book is Lorena.

20. "Freedom In Your Love" words and music by Joyce Lichtenberger © 1988. Used by permission.

About the Author

For three decades Hugo Neufeld served as a leader at Welcome Inn, a community center and church in one of the poorest neighborhoods of Hamilton, Ontario. He holds a bachelor's degree in theology from Canadian Mennonite Bible College and a bachelor's in sociology from Bethel College. He earned a master of social work from University of Toronto in 1968, and a master of divinity from Associated Mennonite Biblical Seminary in 1990.

At Welcome Inn, Hugo and his wife, Doreen, were both ordained to pastoral ministry. After leaving the Welcome Inn in 1989, they continued their co-ministry as Mission Ministers for Mennonite Church Eastern Canada. They eventually moved to Calgary, where they co-pastored Trinity Mennonite Church. They retired from full-time pastoral work in 2004 and remain involved in various types of ministry, including intercultural work.